FCE
Practice Tests

Four tests for the FCE exam

MARK HARRISON

OXFORD
UNIVERSITY PRESS

OXFORD
UNIVERSITY PRESS

Great Clarendon Street, Oxford OX2 6DP

Oxford University Press is a department of the University of Oxford.
It furthers the University's objective of excellence in research, scholarship,
and education by publishing worldwide in

Oxford New York

Auckland Cape Town Dar es Salaam Hong Kong Karachi
Kuala Lumpur Madrid Melbourne Mexico City Nairobi
New Delhi Shanghai Taipei Toronto

With offices in

Argentina Austria Brazil Chile Czech Republic France Greece
Guatemala Hungary Italy Japan Poland Portugal Singapore
South Korea Switzerland Thailand Turkey Ukraine Vietnam

OXFORD and OXFORD ENGLISH are registered trade marks of
Oxford University Press in the UK and in certain other countries

ACKNOWLEDGEMENTS

*The author and publisher are grateful to those who have given permission to reproduce
the following extracts and adaptations of copyright material:* p6 'Hi, anxiety' by
Tiffany Hancock; Daily Telegraph, 14/01/06. Reproduced by permission
of Telegraph Media Group Ltd. p8 'Want to join the jet-set?' by Linda
Whitney; Daily Mail, 30/03/06. Reproduced by permission of Daily Mail.
p14 'Multi-tasking children are losing the plot' by John Elliot; The Sunday
Times, 26/03/06. © NI Syndication. p20 'Where picking up the ball with a
trunk …' by the Duke of Argyll; Daily Telegraph, 29/11/2006. Reproduced
by permission of Telegraph Media Group Ltd. p26 Extract from the novel
A Gathering Light by Jennifer Donnelly. Reproduced by permission of
Bloomsbury publishers. p28 'The Tower and the Glory' by Chris Wilson;
Daily Telegraph, 10/09/05. Reproduced by permission of Telegraph Media
Group Ltd. p31 'Wheels that changed the world' by Nick Horley; Daily Mail,
09/05/05. Reproduced by permission of Daily Mail. p39 'Power to the people'
by David Derbyshire; Daily Telegraph, 04/11/2006. Reproduced by permission
of Telegraph Media Group Ltd. p46 'Are you on the right track?' by Frances
Childs; Daily Telegraph, 18/08/05. Reproduced by permission of Telegraph
Media Group Ltd. p51 'Smart art' by Sean Newsom; The Sunday Times,
19/06/2005. © NI Syndicationp62 'Our girls are alive with the Sound of Music'
by Hugh Davies, Daily Telegraph, 14/10/2006. Reproduced by permission of
Telegraph Media Group Ltd. p66 'Why I've taken a break from holidays' by
Tom Cox, Daily Telegraph 18/08/05. Reproduced by permission of Telegraph
Media Group Ltd. p78 '24 Hours in Food' by Kate Salter; The Sunday Times,
November, 2006. © NI Syndication. p79 'Dashboard dunces are exposed'
by Sally Pook; Daily Telegraph, 03/03/2006. Reproduced by permission of
Telegraph Media Group Ltd. p80 'Change your life in 60 seconds' by Louise
Armitstead; The Times, 19/06/05. © NI Syndication

Sources: Hendon & Finchley Times

*Although every effort has been made to trace and contact copyright holders before
publication, this has not been possible in some cases. We apologize for any apparent
infringement of copyright and if notified, the publisher will be pleased to rectify any
errors or omissions at the earliest opportunity.*

The publisher would like to thank the following for permission to reproduce photographs:
Alamy pp8 (JupiterimagesPolka Dot), 28 (Con O'Donoghue), 31 (The Print
Collector), 121bl (Sindre Ellingsen), 121br (Janine Wiedel Photolibrary),
121tr (ETCbild), 124tl (Felipe Rodriguez), 124tr (Andrew Butterton), 125bl
(PhotoAlto), 125tr (JLImages), 127bl (picturesbyrob), 127br (Neil Setchfield);
Corbis UK Ltd. pp51 (Sandro Vannini), 71b (Cynthia Hart Designer),
71c;71t;124bl (Medioimages), 124br (Randy Faris), 125tl (Fancy/Veer), 127tr
(Thinkstock); Daily Telegraph p6 (Martin Pope); Fotolibra p121tl (Peter
Cope); Getty Images pp48 (Tariq Dajani), 68 (Newsmakers), 124bcr (Barry
Willis), 124tcr (Christopher Furlong); iStockphoto pp123br (Sean Locke),
127tl (Chris Schmidt); Oxford University Press pp124tc (Photodisc), 125br
(Creatas); Photolibrary Group p123bl;Random House p11;Rex Features
pp123ccl (c.20thC.Fox/Everett), 123ccr (Dreamworks/Everett), 123cl (c.20thC.
Fox/Everett), 123cr (c.Dreamworks/Everett), 123tl (c.20thC.Fox/Everett), 123tr
(c.Dreamworks/Everett)

Illustrations by: Mark Duffin: pp 122, 126; David Eaton: p 128

Contents

Introduction

This book contains:

- four complete Practice Tests for the Cambridge First Certificate in English
- answer key, including mark schemes for all Writing tasks
- model answers for all Writing tasks
- guide to marking, including Do-it-yourself marksheets
- guidance on how to assess the Writing and Speaking papers
- sample answer sheets
- audio scripts

Exam content

Paper 1: Reading (1 hour)

	Text	Question type	Focus
PART 1	1 text (article, fiction, non-fiction)	4-option multiple choice	comprehension of detail, gist, opinion, attitude, purpose, reference, exemplification, comparison, main idea, tone; deducing meaning **8 questions; 16 marks**
PART 2	1 text with 7 sentences missing	choice of 8 sentences to fill the gaps	understanding of text structure, links between parts of text **7 questions; 14 marks**
PART 3	1 text divided into sections OR several short texts	matching statements / information to section of text or short text they refer to or appear in	location of specific information / points; comprehension of paraphrasing **15 questions; 15 marks**

Paper 2: Writing (1 hour 20 minutes)

	Task	Focus
PART 1	letter or email using given notes (120–150 words). Candidates **must** do this task.	advising, apologizing, comparing, describing, explaining, expressing opinions, justifying, persuading, recommending, suggesting **20 marks**
PART 2	article, essay, report, review, story or letter (120–180 words) Questions 2–4: candidates choose one task from three choices OR Questions 5a/5b: candidates may choose one task about the set books. (There are two set books and these change from time to time; therefore in this book, the set book tasks are generalized.)	varying according to the task, including advising, comparing, describing, explaining, expressing opinions, justifying, recommending **20 marks**

Paper 3: Use of English (45 minutes)

	Text / Input	Question type	Focus
PART 1	1 short text with 12 gaps	4-option multiple-choice; choose the correct word(s) to fill each gap	vocabulary (meaning of single words, completion of phrases, phrasal verbs, etc.) 12 questions; 12 marks
PART 2	1 short text with 12 gaps	fill each gap with one word	mostly grammar, some vocabulary 12 questions; 12 marks
PART 3	1 short text with 10 gaps	use the words given to form the correct word for each gap	word formation 10 questions; 10 marks
PART 4	8 unrelated sentences, each followed by a single word and a gapped sentence	use the word given to complete the gapped sentence so that it means the same as the first sentence	grammar and vocabulary 8 questions; 16 marks *(1 mark for each part of the answer, max. 2 marks per question)*

Paper 4: Listening (40 minutes)

In the exam, each recording is heard twice. On the CD, Parts 2, 3 and 4 are not repeated and the track will need to be played again. At the end of the exam, candidates are given 5 minutes to transfer their answers to the answer sheet.

	Recording	Question type	Focus
PART 1	8 short pieces (monologue or conversation)	3-option multiple-choice (1 question per piece)	detail, gist, opinion, attitude, function, purpose, situation, topic, genre, relationship, speaker, addressee, place 8 questions; 8 marks
PART 2	1 monologue or conversation	sentence completion: 10 sentences to complete with a word or short phrase	understanding of specific information given in the piece 10 questions; 10 marks
PART 3	5 short monologues	matching: match what each speaker says to 1 of 6 options	as Part 1 5 questions; 5 marks
PART 4	1 interview or discussion (2 or more speakers) OR 1 monologue	3-option multiple-choice	understanding of detail, gist, opinion, attitude 7 questions; 7 marks

Paper 5: Speaking (14 minutes)

	Activity type (examiner + two candidates)	Focus
PART 1	conversation between candidates and examiner (3 mins)	general and personal topics relating to the candidate
PART 2	individual 'long turn' for each candidate with a brief response from second candidate (4 mins)	candidates talk about 2 sets of 2 pictures
PART 3	2-way conversation between candidates (3 mins)	candidates discuss a situation described in words and pictures in order to reach conclusions
PART 4	conversation between candidates and examiner (4 mins)	candidates discuss topics related to Part 3 task with the examiner 20 marks total

All papers have equal value: 20% of the total. For a guide to calculating marks, see pages 91-92.

Paper 1: Reading (1 hour)

You are going to read a newspaper article about an adventure centre. For questions 1–8, choose the answer (A, B, C or D) which you think fits best according to the text.

Mark your answers on the separate answer sheet.

A family adventure centre

I'm focused. Completely terrified, but focused. I've got a tiny area to stand on and beneath me is a 10-metre drop. To make things worse, the totem pole that I'm trying to climb onto is shaking. With one knee bent on the top of the pole and the other foot next to it, I slowly stand up with my arms outstretched for balance. Once upright, my legs are still wobbling but an enormous smile has spread across my face. I shuffle my toes over the edge. And then I jump. Back on the ground, my knees won't stop quaking. But for the boys at Head 4 Heights, an aerial adventure centre in Cirencester, it's all in a day's work.

Head 4 Heights, one of the tallest climbing centres in Britain, opened two years ago. It's the only UK climbing centre open to the public year-round (the only days it closes are when winds exceed 70 mph, almost enough to blow you off a totem pole and into one of the lakes). The course was set up by Rod Baber, adventurer extraordinaire and holder of the world record for scaling the highest peak of every country in Europe in the shortest time. Rod's latest plan is to snag the record for North and South America as well, but in between he starts every day with a clamber round the Cirencester course. His favourite is the 'Trapeze' challenge: 'It still gets me every time. Eyes dilate,

mouth goes dry and adrenalin goes everywhere.'

Although the course is only roughly the size of a tennis court, it packs a lot into a small space. There are four totem poles (of varying degrees of difficulty according to the holds attached to them), a stairway to heaven (a giant ladder with an increasing distance between the rungs), two freefall platforms and a trapeze jump. Plans for a new 30-metre pole are presently under way. All can be made easier or harder, according to ability, and incorporated into different challenges, which is why the course has proved a success with families, corporate days out and the armed forces. More than half who visit return for more and the centre now averages about 1,500 visitors a month.

All ages over five are welcome, but children are the most enthusiastic and 'far easier to teach than the bankers,' says Rod. Parents are usually more reluctant to join in. 'We hear all sorts of excuses,' says Rod. 'Everything from bad knees to "I haven't trimmed my toenails".' The oldest customer was a 78-year-old who arrived with his son and grandson. When the younger two decided to give it a miss, the grandfather set off to show them how it was done.

For the most part, though, people start off nervous and only

gain confidence as they progress. 'Everything is kept very positive. We always tell people to look up not down and to take their time,' says Rod. 'We want to push people outside their comfort zone and into the adventure zone, but we don't want people to be pushed into the panic zone, which can be mentally damaging.'

Also reassuring is the 100 per cent safety record. The course was designed and built by Nick Moriarty, an expert in his field who has constructed 450 courses in 16 countries and trained 2,700 instructors. Key to the design is the safety-rope system, which ensures that if you do lose your balance or grip, your full-body harness will guarantee that you float, not fall, back to earth.

What isn't guaranteed, though, is family harmony. 'The Leap of Love' is usually left as the final challenge and involves two (similarly sized) people squeezing themselves onto a 'bird table' at the top of a totem pole, before jumping in tandem to grab a trapeze. Not everything always goes according to plan. Aside from not arguing, both people need to be careful not to unbalance each other and must jump at exactly the same time. 'We do have some people who have refused to speak to each other afterwards,' says Rod, 'but if you can both make it together, it's such a buzz.'

1 One problem the writer describes in the first paragraph is that
   A she keeps falling off the totem pole.
   B she is trying to stand on top of a moving object.
   C she cannot get her arms into the right position.
   D she is too nervous to complete the climb.

1

2 What do we learn about Head 4 Heights in the second paragraph?
   A It remains open even in quite windy conditions.
   B Rod Baber got the idea for it while climbing mountains.
   C It did not initially stay open throughout the year.
   D It is aimed at people who don't have the chance to climb mountains.

2

3 What does Rod Baber say about the 'Trapeze' challenge?
   A He does it more often than anything else on the course.
   B He always fails to complete it.
   C He continues to find it difficult.
   D He takes a long time to recover after doing it.

3

4 The writer says that the main reason for the course's popularity is that
   A the challenges it offers cannot be found anywhere else.
   B new challenges are constantly being added.
   C it can be completed in a fairly short time.
   D it can be adapted for different people.

4

5 The people who 'decided to give it a miss' (column 2) are examples of people who
   A find it difficult to do the course.
   B are unwilling to do the course.
   C are easily taught how to do the course.
   D give up while they are doing course.

5

6 Rod says that the intention of the course is that people taking part
   A learn how to deal with extreme fear.
   B progress as quickly as possible.
   C take risks they might not initially want to take.
   D increase in confidence after repeated visits.

6

7 The writer uses the phrase 'Also reassuring' (column 3) to emphasize
   A that people benefit from doing the course.
   B how carefully the course has been constructed.
   C that people should not be afraid to do the course.
   D how enthusiastic Rod is about the course.

7

8 What is said about 'The Leap of Love'?
   A Most people fail to do it successfully.
   B It can cause people to fall out with each other.
   C It is the hardest challenge on the course.
   D Some people don't try hard enough to do it.

8

You are going to read an article about jobs that involve international travel. Seven sentences have been removed from the article. Choose from the sentences A–H the one which fits each gap (9–15). There is one extra sentence which you do not need to use.

Mark your answers on the separate answer sheet.

WANT TO JOIN THE JET SET?

You could be jetting off to exotic locations, staying in five-star hotels, eating in top-class restaurants, and it's all paid for by your employer. Who wouldn't want a job that involves foreign travel? **9**_____ The number of jobs requiring international travel is growing significantly. And citing business travel experience on your CV can bring enormous professional benefits.

But it's not always as exciting as it sounds. There is a big difference between travelling to Milan as a tourist and travelling there to spend a day in the type of hotel meeting room that can be found anywhere in Europe. It can be very exciting, but you need to keep your feet firmly on the ground. **10**_____ Flights can be delayed, things can go wrong and it's easy to get exhausted. Many jobs mean travelling alone, so you can be lonely.

Simply targeting any job that involves foreign travel is not the way to start. **11**_____ It's as illogical as saying you want a job that involves wearing smart clothes. Instead, you should consider all the usual factors, such as qualifications and experience, and only then choose a sector or company that offers opportunities for international travel.

The travel and hotel trades are obvious areas, but the commercial sector also offers good prospects for travel. In the retail sector, buyers often travel, especially if they work in fresh produce, where they have to check the suitability of crops. **12**_____ Jobs in the engineering and environment sector can involve travel, too. Almost any career can mean international travel, if you choose the right company and role. The number of jobs involving travel, especially at middle-management level, is growing.

So what will help you secure a role with an international flavour? **13**_____ A second language is a good indication of how well someone will adapt. You need to show you are flexible and willing to learn. If your company has a sister company in the Czech Republic, for instance, learning some Czech will boost your chances.

Find out what the company offers as a support package. Many now guarantee that you can return home at the weekends, or they will limit the amount that people travel each year. **14**_____ One company asked graduates fresh out of university to move to another country over a weekend, alone, and to find their own accommodation.

And it's as well to remember that international travel can be stressful. People can get burned out by international business travel. You need to be in control of your schedule, rather than leaving it to the company. You must ensure you get time to rest and talk to your employer all the time about how you are coping. Don't wait for formal appraisals or until they ask for your views. **15**_____ Most sensible companies ask people to commit to two to three years. This increases the likelihood of success. And most people who travel on business remember it fondly.

A On the other hand, it does bring personal benefits, and it also has a dramatic effect on promotion prospects.

B Making travel your first requirement is not the way to choose a career.

C And realize you might not want to travel for ever.

D Employers look for candidates with an international outlook.

E And there are plenty of opportunities.

F But not all employers are like this.

G Speak to seasoned international business travellers to get an idea of what you will face.

H Employment in communications, banking and finance, and property management is also worth looking at.

You are going to read a magazine article about various authors. For questions 16–30, choose from the authors (A–D). The authors may be chosen more than once.

Mark your answers on the separate answer sheet.

Which author

feels that she is not completely in control when she is writing?	16
took action in response to someone's negative view of her chances of getting her work accepted?	17
thinks that her current working arrangement may not be permanent?	18
decides when information given in her books does not have to be true?	19
did something dishonest while trying to get her work accepted?	20
is unwilling to do a great deal of background work for her books?	21
was offered her first contract as a result of an earlier success?	22
makes sure that her books contain strange elements?	23
got great pleasure from carrying out a certain process repeatedly?	24
draws attention to the likelihood of a new author getting their work accepted?	25
wants people to be cheered up by her books?	26
feels that it is an advantage that people give her their sincere views on her work?	27
recommends analysing various aspects of other authors' books?	28
leaves sentences incomplete while she is writing?	29
felt that her job was taking up too much of her attention?	30

TEST 1

The best-sellers book club

Fancy being an author? We asked some of Britain's favourite best-selling writers to share the secrets of their success.

A JOANNE HARRIS *Her novels have attracted millions of fans worldwide.*

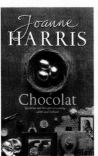

MY BIG BREAK I was a full-time teacher and made time to write my first novel before and after school. It took two years. Then I spent a fortune on posting manuscripts to agents. I found one, but he got discouraged when my manuscripts were rejected, so I sacked him and wrote my next novel, which my next agent loved. He got me a deal for both novels.

HOW I WORK I travel a lot, on promotional work, but when I'm at home I work in my library, looking out onto the garden. I don't want to do lots of research, so I stick to subjects I know about.

MY BEST ADVICE 100,000 titles are published in the UK every year. For each, 100 are rejected. If, knowing this, you still want to write and you love it, you're on the right track.

THE SECRET OF MY SUCCESS I don't believe in a magic wand. You need ability, luck and hard work.

B LAUREN CHILD *She writes and illustrates children's books for two to 10-year-olds.*

MY BIG BREAK After school, I did an art course. Then I did all sorts of jobs – making lampshades, working as an assistant to artist Damien Hirst (I painted a lot of the spots on his paintings). I wrote my first book in the hope it would become an animation. I found an agent, but didn't get a deal for five years. I didn't lose heart, as so many people were positive about it. Eventually I got a deal and was asked to do a second book.

HOW I WORK In the early days I used to work while I answered the phones at a graphic design agency. Some illustrations take hours, and I prefer having other people around. Now, I've just bought a new house and have a studio, but I'm not sure how long I'll be able to stand working by myself.

MY BEST ADVICE Read as much as you can before you even think of writing. And you can't please everyone – above all, your work must interest you.

THE SECRET OF MY SUCCESS I keep stories simple, but always add a quirky touch – children really like the more bizarre moments in life. I also have a very honest audience who tell me what they think.

C FREYA NORTH *She writes lively, fast-paced fiction.*

MY BIG BREAK I was doing a PhD in Art History and bought a computer. The sheer joy of typing then deleting stuff was compulsive and I started to write fiction that I actually wanted to read. After four years of rejections, I presumed I was doing something wrong. Then I worked for a publishing company and realized I needed an agent. I sent my manuscript with fake reviews I'd made up myself to lots of agents. One took me on and got me a three-book deal.

HOW I WORK I used to work at our kitchen table, but now I go to the library. Touch-typing was the best thing I ever learnt. I never interrupt the flow and just throw in asterisks if I can't think of an adjective. It's as if the story and the characters have taken me over and I have to struggle to keep up!

MY BEST ADVICE Let your character dictate the story. It could be the most intricate plot in the world, but if the characters aren't 'real', no one will care.

THE SECRET OF MY SUCCESS I write simply and keep chapters short so my readers can enjoy them on journeys home at the end of a bad day. I want them to giggle.

D MANDA SCOTT *She has written a cult series of historical novels.*

MY BIG BREAK I was a veterinary anaesthetist. On my 30th birthday, I was climbing a mountain and I was happy, but all I could think about was work on Monday. I decided to follow my heart and make a living from writing. I was among the finalists in a writing competition and from that got a deal for my first book.

HOW I WORK I have a routine: in the morning, edit everything from the previous day, then I walk my dogs and write in the afternoon.

MY BEST ADVICE Read bad books and work out what makes them bad. Read the books you love and work out why you love them. Write what you will really, really want to read. Always.

THE SECRET OF MY SUCCESS I'm good at judging what needs to be factual and what I can make up.

Paper 2: Writing (1 hour 20 minutes)

PART 1

*You **must** answer this question. Write your answer in 120–150 words in an appropriate style.*

1   You are going to visit Britain for three weeks in the near future. You have received an email from a British friend, Olivia, about some relatives of hers who you can visit during your stay. Read Olivia's email and the notes you have made. Then write a letter to Olivia's relatives, using **all** your notes.

---

email   **page 1 of 1**

From: Olivia Wood
Sent: 21st June
Subject: Your visit

I've just had an idea about your trip here next month. While you're here, you could visit some relatives of mine who live in the Midlands. I've spoken to them and they'd be pleased to put you up for a few days.

very nice of them

I think you should write to them (name and address below), tell them a little bit about yourself and what you're doing, and fix up the details of your stay with them.

brief description

There are plenty of interesting things to see and do in the area where they live. I'm sure they'll be able to give you some suggestions.

Their details: Mr and Mrs Hampson
                15, Arnold Avenue
                Warwick WK9 6RT

what do they recommend?

suggest dates

Let me know what happens,

Olivia

Write your **letter**. You must use grammatically correct sentences with accurate spelling and punctuation in a style appropriate for the situation.

PART 2

Write an answer to one of the questions 2–5 in this part. Write your answer in 120–180 words in an appropriate style.

2   Your teacher has asked you to write an essay giving your opinion on the following statement.

Computer games are very bad for people and they cause a lot of problems.

Write your **essay**.

3   You have seen this announcement in an international magazine.

> **PERFORMING IN PUBLIC**
>
> Tell us about your experience of performing or speaking in public. What did you do and where? How did it go? Was it a success or a disaster? And how did you feel?
>
> We'll publish the best articles in a special section next month.

Write your **article**.

4   You recently saw this notice in an English-language magazine.

> **WHAT DON'T YOU LIKE ON TV?**
>
> Is there a programme on TV that you really dislike? We're looking for reviews of programmes you really can't stand. Tell us what you don't like about the programme and we'll publish the angriest reviews!

Write your **review**.

5   Answer **one** of the following two questions based on your reading of **one** of the set books.

Either

5(a)   Write an **essay** describing one of the most important events in the book and saying why it is important.

Or

5(b)   Write a **blurb** for the back cover of the book, giving a very brief summary of what it is about and explaining why readers will enjoy it.

Paper 3: Use of English (45 minutes)

PART 1

For questions 1–12, read the text below and decide which answer (A, B, C or D) best fits each gap. There is an example at the beginning (0).

Mark your answers on the separate answer sheet.

Example:

0 **A** seriously   **B** extremely   **C** absolutely   **D** intensely

| 0 | **A** | **B** | **C** | **D** |

Multitasking children

The trend for children to multitask by juggling all sorts of electronic gadgets at the same time is **0**_____ damaging their levels of concentration, scientists have warned. **1**_____ use of the Internet, iPods, mobile phones and DVDs **2**_____ behind that finding. Scientists have **3**_____ the belief of many parents that it is impossible to concentrate on more than one thing at the same time. They found that children **4**_____ homework while sending messages via the Internet can **5**_____ up spending 50% longer than if they had done each task **6**_____ .

David E Meyer, Professor of Cognitive Psychology at the University of Michigan, said that true multitasking is **7**_____ possible for simple activities such as ironing and listening to the radio. He **8**_____ experiments demonstrating that young adults who had to **9**_____ from one maths problem to another wasted significant amounts of time. Meyer said: 'For situations **10**_____ more complex tasks, especially those requiring language, the total time taken to get all the tasks done will increase **11**_____ . Over long periods, this kind of multitasking can stress you out and **12**_____ to mental and physical exhaustion.'

1	**A**	Rocketing	**B**	Heightening	**C**	Ascending	**D**	Leaping
2	**A**	stands	**B**	rests	**C**	lies	**D**	sits
3	**A**	assured	**B**	guaranteed	**C**	authorized	**D**	confirmed
4	**A**	engaging	**B**	tackling	**C**	attending	**D**	undergoing
5	**A**	turn	**B**	come	**C**	use	**D**	end
6	**A**	separately	**B**	distinctly	**C**	apart	**D**	aside
7	**A**	merely	**B**	purely	**C**	only	**D**	simply
8	**A**	set	**B**	put	**C**	took	**D**	ran
9	**A**	alter	**B**	switch	**C**	interrupt	**D**	exchange
10	**A**	consisting	**B**	containing	**C**	involving	**D**	meaning
11	**A**	largely	**B**	greatly	**C**	widely	**D**	highly
12	**A**	result	**B**	proceed	**C**	lead	**D**	bring

PART 2

For questions 13–24, read the text below and think of the word which best fits each gap. Use only one word in each gap. There is an example at the beginning (0).

Write your answers IN CAPITAL LETTERS on the separate answer sheet.

Example:

0	I	T												

The London Marathon

The London Marathon race is a long-running story. **0**_____ was first held in 1981,

13_____ when more than half a million marathon runners of various shapes, sizes and abilities

have completed the challenge of running the full 42 km of the course.

The London Marathon was the brainchild of Chris Brasher. The former Olympic champion brought the

idea home to London **14**_____ completing the New York Marathon in 1979. 'Could London stage

15_____ an event?' wondered Brasher, answering his **16**_____ question by organizing the

first London Marathon on March 29 1981, **17**_____ 6,255 runners completed the course.

The event has captured the public imagination and there are always **18**_____ many people

wanting to take part. Last year **19**_____ amazing 98,500 people applied to run in it, although only

46,500 **20**_____ be accepted.

For most of **21**_____ thousands who do take part, the day is about fun, achievement and raising

money for charity – with varying degrees of pain! It is the immense community spirit that

22_____ the race so special. Clubs, community groups and schools assist and entertain along the

route as the runners – many of **23**_____ in fancy dress – run through the streets raising money for

charitable causes. The streets of London are turned **24**_____ the longest street party in the world as

crowds line the course to cheer the runners and enjoy the spectacle.

For questions 25–34, read the text below. Use the word given in capitals at the end of some of the lines to form a word that fits in the gap in the same line. There is an example at the beginning (0).

Write your answers IN CAPITAL LETTERS on the separate answer sheet.

Example:

0	N	A	T	I	O	N	A	L					

MOBILE LIBRARY'S A WINNER

The city's new mobile library has won an award at a 0 _____ meeting   NATION

of mobile library providers. The award is for the 25 _____ design of   STAND

this new vehicle.

   The stunning external design, which features photographs of people using

libraries, uses the catchphrase 'The Book Stops Here', and co-ordinates

with the attractive 26 _____ leaflets, postcards and posters which give   PUBLIC

details about the library routes and stops.

   The new library went into 27 _____ in April and has been very well   SERVE

received by the public. Both visits and loans of books have increased

28 _____ since the new vehicle began operating. Comments have   CONSIDER

included 'It's such a friendly-looking library', 'I couldn't wait to look

inside!' and 'Thanks for all the 29 _____ new books.'   WONDER

   The mobile library is an air-conditioned, state-of-the-art vehicle, which is

fully networked for using information technology if 30 _____ . The air   REQUIRE

suspension allows the vehicle to be 31 _____ for easy access and ensures   LOW

32 _____ when parked. The internal layout was designed with major   STABLE

input from the library staff, who insisted that the décor was bright and

33 _____ . The library carries up to 3,000 books, CDs and DVDs for   COLOUR

all ages and 34 _____ , and much of the stock is brand new.   INTERESTED

PART 4

For questions 35–42, complete the second sentence so that it has a similar meaning to the first sentence, using the word given. Do not change the word given. You must use between two and five words, including the word given. Here is an example (0).

Example:

0   Making new friends was easy for her.

DIFFICULT

She didn't _____ new friends.

The gap can be filled with the words 'find it difficult to make', so you write:

| 0 | F | I | N | D | | I | T | | D | I | F | F | I | C | U | L | T | | T | O | | M | A | K | E | | |

Write the missing words IN CAPITAL LETTERS on the separate answer sheet.

---

35   Despite winning the race, he wasn't very pleased.

EVEN

He wasn't very pleased, _____ the race.

36   It's a fairly long time since I last watched this programme.

QUITE

I haven't watched this programme _____ time.

37   Were you able to complete all your work yesterday?

GET

Did you manage _____ all your work yesterday?

38   His first novel was better than this one.

GOOD

This novel is not _____ one he wrote.

39   I'm sorry, could you wait for a moment, please?

MIND

I'm sorry, _____ for a moment, please?

40   We're so late now that we definitely won't get to the party on time.

CHANCE

We're so late that we have _____ to the party on time.

41   The food she eats affects her health badly.

EFFECT

The food she eats _____ her health.

42   The only thing I did at the weekend was housework.

APART

I did _____ housework at the weekend.

Paper 4: Listening (40 minutes)

PART 1

You will hear people talking in eight different situations. For questions 1–8, choose the best answer, (A, B or C).

1   You hear someone talking about football referees.
    What is the speaker's attitude towards referees?

    A   They make too many mistakes.

    B   They deserve sympathy.   `1`

    C   Some are better than others.

2   You hear a famous chef talking about his week.
    What does he say about what happened during the week?

    A   He had a problem that was not his fault.

    B   He didn't want to appear on so many programmes.   `2`

    C   He had his first experience of live TV.

3   You hear someone talking about her career in dancing.
    What does she emphasize?

    A   the contribution made by her parents

    B   how much hard work she did   `3`

    C   her desire to be a dancer

4   You hear someone talking on the phone at work.
    Who is she talking to?

    A   a colleague

    B   her boss   `4`

    C   a client

5   You hear a radio presenter talking about a book.
    What feeling does the presenter express about the book?

    A   doubt that it does exactly what it says it does

    B   amazement at how up to date its information is   5

    C   curiosity about how it was written

6   You hear part of an interview with a famous comedian.
    What does he say about his school days?

    A   The teachers never criticized him.

    B   He was only good at one subject.   6

    C   Other people found him amusing.

7   You hear someone talking about a person he knows.
    What is the speaker doing?

    A   complaining

    B   apologizing   7

    C   arguing

8   You hear a tour guide talking to a group of visitors to a museum.
    What does he tell them about the museum?

    A   It's easy to get lost in it.

    B   Big groups aren't allowed in some parts of it.   8

    C   It's better only to visit a small part of it.

PART 2

You will hear someone talking about the sport of elephant polo. For questions 9–18, complete the sentences.

ELEPHANT POLO

Elephants are [_____ 9] animals and so they enjoy elephant polo tournaments.

The [_____ 10] of a goal in elephant polo is the same as in football.

A player and an elephant [_____ 11] both sit on each elephant.

It is against the rules for the elephants to use their trunks to [_____ 12] the ball.

A total of [_____ 13] elephants are required for a game to take place.

The participants are in action for a total of [_____ 14] during each game.

The stick used in the game is both [____ and ____ 15] .

The elephants sometimes want to [_____ 16] in front of a goal.

An elephant with a bad [_____ 17] will be taken out of a game.

African elephants are not used because [_____ 18] cause a problem.

PART 3

You will hear five different people talking about cities they have visited. For questions 19–23, choose from the list (A–F) the opinion each person gives about the city. Use the letters only once. There is one extra letter which you do not need to use.

A   It was exactly as I had imagined.

Speaker 1 [___] **19**

B   It is not as good as it used to be.

Speaker 2 [___] **20**

C   It is hard to find your way around it.

Speaker 3 [___] **21**

D   It is overrated.

Speaker 4 [___] **22**

E   It can get too crowded.

Speaker 5 [___] **23**

F   It was even better than I expected.

PART 4

You will hear an interview with someone who is involved in the music business. For questions 24–30, choose the best answer (A, B or C).

24 What does James say about the radio station he started?
- A Its name was very appropriate.
- B It was more popular than he had expected.
- C It was not very expensive to run.

[24]

25 What does James say about people's attitudes towards his age?
- A They were nicer to him when he was 12 than when he was 16.
- B They were more jealous of him when he was 12 than when he was 16.
- C They expected more of him when he was 16 than when he was 12.

[25]

26 James says that his career in music has included
- A taking over a local radio station.
- B making advertisements.
- C setting up new festivals.

[26]

27 What do we learn about advertising on James' TV channel?
- A There isn't any of it.
- B It always includes music.
- C It doesn't interrupt the programmes.

[27]

28 What does James say about the people interviewed on the channel?
- A They have to say something interesting.
- B They enjoy being interviewed.
- C They often say unexpected things.

[28]

29 What does James say about his ideas?
- A Some of them are not very realistic.
- B He expects to have good ones all the time.
- C He makes sure that he doesn't forget them.

[29]

30 James's advice to listeners who might want to go into business is to
- A forget about past problems.
- B learn from past mistakes.
- C take big risks.

[30]

Paper 5: Speaking (14 minutes)

<u>PART 1</u> (3 minutes)

Where you live

- Where do you live?
- How long have you been living there?
- What kind of building do you live in?
- Who lives with you?
- What do you like / dislike about the town / village / district where you live?

Travel

- Have you been to many other countries? ..... (Which ones?)
- Would you like to travel more? ..... (Where?)
- What's the best country / city / region that you've visited? ..... (Why?)
- Which country / city / region would you most like to visit? ..... (Why?)
- Describe a journey that you often make.

PART 2 (4 minutes)

1 Outdoor activities
2 People's rooms

Candidate A	Look at the two photographs 1A and 1B on page 121. They show people doing outdoor activities. Compare the photographs and say what the people are trying to do. *Candidate A talks on his / her own for about 1 minute.*
Candidate B	Which of the activities would you prefer to do, and why? *Candidate B talks on his / her own for about 20 seconds.*
Candidate B	Look at the two photographs 2A and 2B on page 121. They show people's rooms. Compare the photographs and say whose rooms they might be. *Candidate B talks on his / her own for about 1 minute.*
Candidate A	Which of the rooms is most similar to yours, and in what ways? *Candidate A talks on his / her own for about 20 seconds.*

Exhibitions for a museum

PART 3

Imagine that a local museum is trying to increase visitor numbers. Look at the ideas on page 122 for special exhibitions that are being considered by the museum.

First, talk to each other about how good each of the ideas is. Then decide which two would attract the most visitors to the museum.

Candidates A and B discuss this together for about 3 minutes.

PART 4

- Do you like going to museums or art galleries? ..... (Why / Why not?)
- Which of the subjects interests you the most and which interests you the least? ..... (Why?)
- What are the most well-known museums or art galleries in the place you come from? What do they have in them?
- What kind of things do museums offer to attract young people?
- What is the most interesting museum or art gallery that you've been to? ...... (Why?)
- Which museum or art gallery would you most like to visit? Where is it? What does it have in it? What would you like to see there? ..... (Why?)
- Some people think that museums and art galleries are boring. Do you agree?

Paper 1: Reading (1 hour)

PART 1

You are going to read an extract from a novel. For questions 1–8, choose the answer (A, B, C or D) which you think fits best according to the text.

Mark your answers on the separate answer sheet.

'Afternoon, Mattie!' Mr Eckler called from the bow of his boat. 'Got a new one. Brand-new. Just come in. By a Mrs Wharton. *House of Mirth*, it's called. I tucked it in behind the coffee beans, under *W*. You'll see it.'

'Thank you, Mr Eckler!' I said, excited at the prospect of a new book. 'Did you read it?'

'Yup. Read it whole.'

'What's it about?'

'Can't hardly say. Some flighty city girl. Don't know why it's called *House of Mirth*. It ain't funny in the least.'

The Fulton Chain Floating Library is only a tiny room, a closet really, below decks in Charlie Eckler's pickle boat. It is nothing like the proper library they have in Old Forge, but it has its own element of surprise. Mr Eckler uses the room to store his wares, and when he finally gets around to moving a chest of tea or a sack of cornmeal, you never know what you might find. And once in a while, the main library in Herkimer sends up a new book or two. It's nice to get your hands on a new book before everyone else does. While the pages are still clean and white and the spine hasn't been snapped.

I stepped onto the boat and went below decks. The *House of Mirth* was under *W*, like Mr Eckler said it would be, only it was wedged next to *Mrs Wiggs of the Cabbage Patch*. Mr Eckler sometimes gets authors and titles confused. I signed it out in a ledger he kept on top of a molasses barrel, then rooted around behind a crate of eggs, a jar of marbles and a box of dried dates but found nothing I hadn't already read. I remembered to get the bag of cornmeal we needed. I wished I could buy oatmeal or white flour instead, but cornmeal cost less and went further. I was to get a ten-pound bag. The fifty-pound bag cost more to buy but was cheaper per pound and I'd told Pa so, but he said only rich people can afford to be thrifty.

Just as I was about to climb back upstairs, something caught my eye – a box of composition books. Real pretty ones with hard covers on them, and swirly paint designs, and a ribbon to mark your place. I put the cornmeal down, and Mrs Wharton too, and picked one up. Its pages were smooth and white. I thought it would be a fine thing to write on paper that nice. The pages in my old composition book were rough and had blurry blue lines printed on them, and were made with so little care that there were slivers of wood visible in them.

I handed Mr Eckler fifty cents of my father's money for the cornmeal. 'How much is this?' I asked, holding up one of the pretty composition books. I had sixty cents from all the fiddleheads Weaver and I had sold to the Eagle Bay Hotel. It was money I knew I should have given to my pa. I'd meant to, really. I just hadn't gotten around to it.

'Those notebooks? They're expensive, Mattie. Italians made them. I've got to get forty-five cents apiece,' he said. 'I've got some others coming in for fifteen cents in a week or so if you can wait.'

Forty-five cents was a good deal of money, but I didn't want the ones for fifteen cents, not after I'd seen the others. I had ideas. Tons of them. For stories and poems. I chewed the inside of my cheek, deliberating. I knew I would have to write a lot when I went to Barnard College– *if* I went to Barnard College – and it might be a good idea to get a head start. Weaver had said I should be using my words, not just collecting them, and I knew they would just glide across this beautiful paper, and when I was done writing them, I could close them safely inside the covers. Just like a real book. Guilt gnawed at my insides. I took the money from my pocket and gave it to Mr Eckler quickly, so the thing was done and I couldn't change my mind. Then I watched breathlessly as he wrapped my purchase in brown paper and tied it with string. I thanked him as he handed me the package, but he didn't hear me because Mr Pulling, the station-master, was asking him the price of oranges.

1 When Mr Eckler told Mattie about the new book,

    A Mattie felt that it sounded familiar to her.
    B he said that he thought its title was inappropriate.
    C he said that it was a book Mattie would enjoy.
    D Mattie suspected that he hadn't really read it.

1

2 What does Mattie say about the library in Mr Eckler's boat?

    A New books are frequently added to it.
    B All the books in it are in excellent condition.
    C It contains books that are hidden from view.
    D Mr Eckler doesn't know exactly what is in it.

2

3 When Mattie found the new book, she

    A discovered that there were other new books nearby.
    B saw that it had been put in the wrong place.
    C followed Mr Eckler's system for borrowing books.
    D had to move something so that she could find it.

3

4 What was the situation concerning the cornmeal?

    A Her father was unable to save money by buying the bigger bag.
    B Her father could not see the point of buying the bigger bag.
    C Her father felt that cornmeal was better than oatmeal or white flour.
    D Her father had decided to stop buying what he usually bought.

4

5 One reason why Mattie liked the look of the composition books was that

    A the covers were shiny.
    B the pages were completely clear.
    C the pages were thicker than in her old book.
    D they had better ribbons than her old book.

5

6 When Mattie asked Mr Eckler how much the composition books cost, he said that

    A they weren't really worth the money.
    B they were not the books he had been expecting to receive.
    C he did not expect many people to buy them.
    D he had no choice about how much to charge for them.

6

7 While she was buying one of the books, Mattie thought about

    A how she could use it for making lists of words.
    B what the experience of writing in it would be like.
    C what people at Barnard College would think of it.
    D whether she would have enough ideas to fill the whole book.

7

8 What do we learn about Mattie in the text as a whole?

    A She always thought carefully before making any decisions.
    B She was very keen to impress other people.
    C She was often criticized by people who were close to her.
    D She had an enormous interest in both literature and language.

8

You are going to read an article about an activity in Spain. Seven sentences have been removed from the article. Choose from the sentences A–H the one which fits each gap (9–15). There is one extra sentence which you do not need to use.

Mark your answers on the separate answer sheet.

The Tower and the Glory

Chris Wilson starts at the bottom when he joins a Spanish team making competitive human pyramids

A large man jams his foot in my ear and jumps on to my shoulders. He is quickly followed by another only slightly smaller gentleman who grabs my belt and shimmies up me like a pole. Another follows. My face contorts with pain as the fourth tier mounts on to my back and I begin to sway dangerously. **9** _____ .

'Castelling' (making human castles) is a family sport in Catalonia. Groups normally consist of everyone from tiny children, through awkward adolescents and wiry women, to well-built men at the bottom. **10** _____ I had also heard that being overweight and unfit would not count against me. Sure enough, when I turned up for my first training session, I could sense that, for the first time in years, my ever-expanding physique was being appreciatively looked at.

Castelling began almost 200 years ago near Tarragona, just south of Barcelona. Out of nowhere, it seems that people suddenly began forming themselves into human towers. Since then the sport, if you can call it that, has become an expression of Catalan identity, with groups competing to build ever higher and more elegant structures.

11 _____ Once or twice it has managed a six-tier tower. The top teams regularly manage eight or nine. It was my intention to add a little British beef to the group to help them reach the next level in time for the competitions to be held tomorrow in Barcelona on the National Day of Catalonia.

At first I had thought that I might like to go on top to bask in the glory, but the club's president soon put me straight. He indicated a spindly little girl who looked as though she had been raised entirely on broccoli, and not much of it at that. It is she who has pride of place on top of the pyramid. **12** _____ For my first try-out I was given the role of *segones mans* (second hands), which meant that I supported the wrists of the man who supported the buttocks of the first rank of the pyramid.

Once I had assumed my position, people began to scramble up me and on to the tower without warning. **13** _____ Still, my hard work must have been appreciated because I was quickly promoted to be *primeres mans* and support the bottoms of the first level of the pyramid that we were making under the watchful eye of the artistic director.

My performance in the 'hands' section had obviously been satisfactory because at the third training session I was called forward and given the very great honour of the President's Belt. **14** _____ Being offered this belt, still warm from the very waist of the President, was a clear gesture that me and my bulk had been accepted. Finally, I had made it to the bottom of the pile.

Being a pillar in a castell is much like being a bass player in a band. You know that everyone in the crowd is cheering for the singer or the lead guitarist, no matter how important the rhythm section. When we take the stage tomorrow, no one in the crowd will know who I am, or even be able to see me down at the bottom. All their cheering will be for the little girl on top. **15** _____ It felt great.

A   The best I could hope for was to be at the bottom, but even that honour has to be earned.

B   So I knew that everyone at the training session that night would have cheered with good-natured delight if I had done that.

C   But that memorable night in Figueres, despite the incredible strain, I held steady and the applause was all for me.

D   I had been attracted to castelling because I had been told that it requires almost no skill or co-ordination.

E   Within seconds I had assisted in the formation of a three-tier tower without really noticing what was happening.

F   It's not easy being the bottom man of a human pyramid.

G   Each casteller is wound into a large strip of material worn around the waist to support the back and to help the other castellers grip when they climb.

H   The group I had joined in Figueres, near the French border, is very much a second-division outfit.

You are going to read a magazine article about the history of the bicycle. For questions 16–30, choose from the sections of the article (A–D). The sections may be chosen more than once.

Mark your answers on the separate answer sheet.

In which section of the article are the following mentioned?

features that were not added because they were considered problematic	16
a design that is exactly the same as that of current products	17
a product that became popular despite its price in comparison with an existing product	18
a dramatic reaction to a particular sight	19
a design feature that it was felt would not appeal to men	20
a warning that affected the appeal of a certain product	21
a design that required more than one person to operate the vehicle	22
an attempt to get publicity	23
the possibility of injury because of where the rider sat	24
products that were introduced to compensate for a disadvantage of another product	25
an aspect of design that limited the number of people who could use a certain product	26
a design that some manufacturers felt would not become popular	27
people riding a certain product in order to impress others	28
the motivation of one set of people for changing bicycle design	29
an account of a remarkable achievement	30

Wheels that changed the world

A The bicycle was an absolutely extraordinary creation. Inventors had first begun to wrestle with the challenge of coming up with a human-powered vehicle in the 17th century. In 1696, a French doctor used his manservant to power a pedal-driven carriage while the master sat up front and steered. The beginnings of the modern bicycle emerged in 1818 when Karl von Drais, an eccentric German baron, invented what we now know as the hobbyhorse. It was bicycle-shaped with wooden wheels but had no pedals: the rider had to push it forward with his feet. At £8 – equivalent today to £500 – the hobbyhorse could be afforded only by true gentlemen, and it soon became a much sought-after status symbol. But the craze died out after a year following a statement from the London College of Surgeons, which said darkly that the hobbyhorse could cause 'internal injuries'.

B Brilliant minds continued to wrestle with the mechanical horse but made slow progress. Even Britain's top engineer, Isambard Kingdom Brunel, could come up with nothing better than a hobbyhorse that ran on railway tracks. Finally, in 1887, a Parisian blacksmith called Pierre Michaux added a pair of pedals to a hobbyhorse, and the bicycle was born. The Michaux bicycle had pedals fixed directly to the front wheel, just like a child's tricycle today. Made largely of iron, it weighed as much as a fridge but was easy to ride and took a man up to five miles with the effort he would use to walk only one. Michaux's first newspaper advertisement in May 1867 offered 'pedal velocipedes' for 250 francs. At this price only the wealthy could afford one and a group of 20 young men spent their days showing off their 'steeds' before fascinated crowds in the Bois de Boulogne. Michaux was soon producing 20 bicycles a day, and decided to organize a women's race as a stunt to boost his sales further. A racecourse in Bordeaux was roped off, but when the four lady racers made their appearance in short skirts, the crowd of 3,000 burst through the barriers. Nevertheless, the ladies raced off. A contemporary report recorded that Miss Louise took an early lead, but Miss Julie made a 'superhuman effort', passing her on the home straight and winning by a nose. Within a year, there were 50,000 bicycles in France.

C Not to be outdone by their French counterparts, British engineers set about improving bicycle design with wire-spoked wheels and solid rubber tyres. The weight was reduced to a mere 44lb, only twice the weight of a bike today. Gears and chains were still thought too heavy and complex to be fitted to a bicycle, so designers could increase top speed only by increasing the size of the front wheel. Eventually front wheels grew until they were 5ft and the penny farthing was born. Speeds of 20 mph were now possible, but the rider's seat was directly above the front wheel, which made riding in a skirt impossible, so women were effectively barred from bicycles. To make up for it, manufacturers developed tricycles with low seats. The penny farthing's biggest drawback was its danger: the high seat was difficult to climb into, and once up there the driver had a long way to fall.

D In 1885, John Starley launched the Rover Safety Bicycle, the first model to adopt what we now think of as the traditional design. The bicycle industry was unimpressed, as it had a chain-driven rear wheel, which added weight, and a low seat, which made male riders look a bit ridiculous. But it turned out to be faster than a penny farthing because it was more aerodynamic. More importantly, the Rover could be ridden in a skirt. At £22, it was more expensive than a penny farthing, but its practicality was just what the public wanted. Soon there were half a million bicycles in the UK. Between 1890 and 1900, the bicycle was refined until the basic design became very similar to the featherweights that modern champions ride in the Tour de France. Lightweight steel tubing, the diamond-shaped frame, gears and pneumatic tyres with separate inner tubes all became common. Top speeds of 25 mph could now be reached. At last the cyclist could outrun a galloping horse. The bicycle was found in every walk of life: policemen and postmen had them and several European armies issued them to their soldiers.

Paper 2: Writing (1 hour 20 minutes)

PART 1

You must *answer this question. Write your answer in 120–150 words in an appropriate style.*

1 You have received an email from your English-speaking friend, George. Read George's email and the notes you have made. Then write an email to George, using **all** your notes.

---

email	page 1 of 1

From: George Cooper
Sent: 10th November
Subject: Problems, problems

I'm not having the best of times at the moment. This seems to be one of those periods when things are going wrong. *→ express sympathy*

First of all, I've got so much to do at work that I don't know how I'm going to get it all done. I used to enjoy the job, but now I'm under terrible pressure and it's really getting me down. *→ do something about this!*

On top of that, I've had a big argument with Helen, and she says she doesn't want to see me any more. It was a stupid argument, and I said things I didn't mean. We've been going out together for nearly a year, and I don't want to split up with her. *suggest solution*

Sorry to be so miserable. Write to me soon. *cheer up!*

George

Write your **email**. You must use grammatically correct sentences with accurate spelling and punctuation in a style appropriate for the situation.

PART 2

Write an answer to one *of the questions 2–5 in this part. Write your answer in 120–180 words in an appropriate style.*

2   You recently saw this notice in an international magazine.

> ### LOCAL REPORTERS WANTED!
>
> We're looking for people to send us reports on what has been happening in their village, city or region over the past year. You can tell us about important events, ordinary day-to-day life, people in general or specific individuals.
>
> We'll publish some of the reports in a special section.

Write your report.

3   Your teacher has asked you to write a story for an international magazine. The story must end with the following words:

After that, Tom promised himself that he would never make the same mistake again.

Write your story.

4   You have seen this announcement in an English-language magazine.

> ### FANCY YOURSELF AS AN INTERVIEWER?
>
> Is there someone that you'd like to interview? It doesn't have to be a living person. Write and tell us who you'd like to interview if you had the chance. Why would you like to interview that person? What would you ask? We'll publish the best letters in the next issue.

Write your letter.

5   Answer one of the following two questions based on your reading of one of the set books.

Either

5(a) Which characters do you like and dislike most in the book? Write an essay describing those characters and giving reasons for your choices.

Or

5(b) Write a review of the book for other people who are learning English. Write about any good or bad aspects for people learning the language, and say whether or not you recommend it to other learners, giving reasons.

Paper 3: Use of English (45 minutes)

PART 1

For questions 1–12, read the text below and decide which answer (A, B, C or D) best fits each gap. There is an example at the beginning (0).

Mark your answers on the separate answer sheet.

Example:

0 **A** granting   **B** appreciating   **C** rewarding   **D** distributing

0	A	B	C	D
	‿	‿	▬	‿

Britain's first shopping centre

Brent Cross Shopping Centre in London recently celebrated its 30th anniversary, 0_____ 36 staff who have worked there since it opened with gifts. Brent Cross was the first large-scale indoor shopping centre in Britain and many 1_____ it would be a 2_____ failure. Instead, the centre, with its 75 stores, started a shopping 3_____ in Britain.

'They said it 4_____ no chance of becoming popular, but in the first week it was packed, you couldn't move in here, and that's how it's 5_____ on,' said George Dorman, 68, who has been working as a fruit and vegetable sales assistant at the Waitrose store since it opened. 'It's a 6_____ achievement and I've enjoyed every

7_____ minute of it,' he said. 'The company has been very supportive and they help you 8_____ . It's a very secure job.'

Sisters Jeanette Harris and Lydia Neidus have both been working as sales assistants at the Fenwicks store since the centre opened. Ms Neidus said: 'The more you get involved, the more you 9_____ to love it because you've seen everything and you've 10_____ so much knowledge about it all.' Her sister added: 'It's just the most wonderful achievement. I mean, I 11_____ as if it was 12_____ yesterday when I started and I've loved every minute. The proof of that is that I'm still here and still working.'

1	**A** estimated	**B** awaited	**C** assessed	**D** predicted
2	**A** whole	**B** complete	**C** full	**D** true
3	**A** novelty	**B** alteration	**C** conversion	**D** revolution
4	**A** took	**B** stood	**C** ran	**D** held
5	**A** stayed	**B** carried	**C** moved	**D** stuck
6	**A** great	**B** high	**C** large	**D** vast
7	**A** actual	**B** single	**C** individual	**D** separate
8	**A** up	**B** on	**C** out	**D** off
9	**A** develop	**B** reach	**C** grow	**D** arrive
10	**A** increased	**B** gained	**C** raised	**D** expanded
11	**A** feel	**B** seem	**C** sense	**D** find
12	**A** quite	**B** simply	**C** hardly	**D** just

*For questions 13–24, read the text below and think of the word which best fits each gap. Use only **one** word in each gap. There is an example at the beginning (0).*

Write your answers IN CAPITAL LETTERS on the separate answer sheet.

Example:

0	H	O	W										

See dinosaurs eating!

Dinosaurs died out more than 60 million years ago, so **0**_____ on earth can we tell what they used to eat? Find out at the Cameron Museum, where you can step **13**_____ in time and join some dinosaurs enjoying their lunch. **14**_____ you enter the new Meet the Dinosaurs exhibition, you'll meet four full-size dinosaur heads, **15**_____ of them munching away on their favourite food. The model dinosaurs are **16**_____ realistic that you could easily forget that they're **17**_____ real.

Scientists have pieced **18**_____ information from fossils to work out that dinosaurs with large claws and sharp teeth ate meat, while flatter teeth were used **19**_____ grinding plants. So Tyrannosaurus rex, with its prehistoric table manners **20**_____ teeth as sharp as razors, might not have been the **21**_____ relaxing dinner guest!

But, **22**_____ you're a meat eater or a vegetarian, **23**_____ not come along to the exhibition and **24**_____ sure you don't miss an incredible day out!

PART 3

For questions 25–34, read the text below. Use the word given in capitals at the end of some of the lines to form a word that fits in the gap in the same line. *There is an example at the beginning* (0).

Write your answers IN CAPITAL LETTERS *on the separate answer sheet.*

Example:

| 0 | C | H | A | L | L | E | N | G | I | N | G | | |

ESCORTED TOURS

Organizing a holiday can be a very **0** _____ task. Some people find   CHALLENGE

the experience as **25** _____ as the daily demands of work and family   STRESS

26 _____ . If you are in this situation, you may find that taking an   COMMIT

escorted holiday is the ideal **27** _____ .   SOLVE

    Escorted holidays offer a great balance between sightseeing, entertainment

and leisure time, with the added advantage that you have the services of a

professional tour manager, who **28** _____ you throughout the trip,   COMPANY

acting as your **29** _____ guide. From the first day to the last, tour   PERSON

managers make your holiday experience even more **30** _____ because   MEMORY

of the invaluable information and **31** _____ suggestions they provide.   HELP

Your tour manager will give you many **32** _____ into the place you are   SIGHT

visiting, including useful information on the **33** _____ characteristics   DISTINCT

of the place, such as regional food and local entertainment.

    If you book one of the escorted holiday packages that we offer, you can be

sure that you will have a **34** _____ authentic travel experience.   TRUE

TEST 2

For questions 35–42, complete the second sentence so that it has a similar meaning to the first sentence, using the word given. Do not change the word given. *You must use between* two *and* five *words, including the word given. Here is an example (0).*

Example:

0   Making new friends was easy for her.

DIFFICULT

She didn't _____ new friends.

The gap can be filled with the words 'find it difficult to make', so you write:

| 0 | F | I | N | D | | I | T | | D | I | F | F | I | C | U | L | T | | T | O | | M | A | K | E | | |

Write the missing words IN CAPITAL LETTERS *on the separate answer sheet.*

35   He didn't buy a present for her, he gave her some money.

INSTEAD

He gave her some money _____ present.

36   A temporary manager is running the shop at the moment.

RUN

The shop _____ a temporary manager at the moment.

37   If you keep trying, you'll improve.

GIVE

If you _____ , you'll get better.

38   How long is your journey from home to work?

TAKE

How long _____ get from home to work?

39   When I rang the box office, the tickets had all been sold.

LEFT

There _____ when I rang the box office.

40   I was surprised when I discovered the truth.

FIND

I was surprised _____ the truth was.

41   If public opinion doesn't change suddenly, he'll win the next election.

SUDDEN

Unless _____ change in public opinion, he'll win the next election.

42   This is the happiest that Paula has ever been.

HAPPIER

Paula _____ she is now.

Paper 4: Listening (40 minutes)

PART 1

You will hear people talking in eight different situations. For questions 1–8, choose the best answer (A, B or C).

1 You hear part of an interview with a sportsman.
  What does he say about playing for the national team?

   A He doesn't think it will happen soon.

   B It isn't his main concern at the moment.   **1**

   C The possibility of it happening has put him under pressure.

2 You hear the introduction to a radio programme.
  What is the speaker doing?

   A contrasting weather forecasting in the past and the present

   B explaining why weather forecasting has become more accurate   **2**

   C joking about how people used to forecast the weather

3 You hear a man talking about reading aloud to children.
  What opinion does he express?

   A Short stories are better than longer books.

   B The choice of book may not be important.   **3**

   C It's hard to know what will make children laugh.

4 You hear someone talking about work.
  What is his situation?

   A He has just left a job.

   B He is thinking of leaving his job.   **4**

   C He has just started a new job.

5   You hear someone talking about his childhood.
    What does he mention?

    A   a habit he regards as strange

    B   regret about some of his behaviour   [ ] **5**

    C   how much he has changed

6   You hear someone talking about something that happened at a party.
    How did the speaker feel?

    A   upset

    B   amused   [ ] **6**

    C   frightened

7   You hear part of a talk about blues music.
    What is the speaker talking about?

    A   why it originated in a certain area

    B   how popular it was in the past compared with today   [ ] **7**

    C   its importance in the history of popular music

8   You hear someone on the radio talking about a website for consumers.
    What is the speaker's purpose?

    A   to encourage consumers to make complaints

    B   to inform consumers about a source of information   [ ] **8**

    C   to describe common problems for consumers

PART 2

You will hear a radio interview about indoor skydiving. For questions 9–18, complete the sentences.

INDOOR SKYDIVING

The fans in the tunnel are normally used for putting air into [_____ **9**] .

It has been said that the machine looks like a huge [_____ **10**] .

The walls in the tunnel are made of [_____ **11**] .

The only parts of the body that can get hurt in the tunnel are the
[_____ and _____ **12**] .

You have to be [_____ **13**] years old to use the tunnel.

You have to wear [_____ **14**] when you use the tunnel.

Beginners have two [_____ **15**] lessons in the tunnel with an instructor.

During lessons, you get into a position as if you have a [_____ **16**] in your hands.

The person who created the wind tunnel refers to it as a '[_____ **17**]'.

Indoor skydiving has become a sport called [_____ **18**] .

You will hear five different people talking about the reasons why they became very successful. For questions 19–23, choose from the list (A–F) the reason each person gives for their success. Use the letters only once. There is one extra letter which you do not need to use.

A   natural ability

Speaker 1 ☐ **19**

B   encouragement from others

Speaker 2 ☐ **20**

C   careful planning

Speaker 3 ☐ **21**

D   constant good luck

Speaker 4 ☐ **22**

E   determination to improve

Speaker 5 ☐ **23**

F   lack of competition

You will hear someone giving a talk about taking up running as an activity. For questions 24–30, choose the best answer (A, B or C).

24 The speaker says that when she was younger,
    A she envied people who did a lot of physical activity.
    B she knew that she ought to take up some kind of physical activity.   **24**
    C she hated the idea of doing any kind of physical activity.

25 The speaker says that if people take up running,
    A she can guarantee that there will be certain benefits.
    B they will wonder why they didn't do it before.   **25**
    C it will become a long-term interest for them.

26 The speaker says that, in comparison with other activities and sports, running is
    A more enjoyable.
    B more convenient.   **26**
    C more beneficial.

27 What does the speaker say about people who feel that they can't take up running?
    A They should talk to people who do run.
    B They may be right.   **27**
    C They know that their attitude is wrong.

28 The speaker warns people who take up running not to
    A be competitive.
    B give up as soon as there is a problem.   **28**
    C ignore pain.

29 What advice does the speaker give about running technique?
    A Change the position of your arms from time to time.
    B Think of your arms as if they were parts of an engine.   **29**
    C Pay more attention to your arms than any other part of your body.

30 What does the speaker say about breathing while running?
    A Some bad advice is sometimes given about it.
    B It takes some time to develop the best technique for it.   **30**
    C There isn't a correct or incorrect way of doing it.

Paper 5: Speaking (14 minutes)

PART 1 (3 minutes)

Family and friends

- Describe briefly the members of your family.
- Describe briefly one or two of your best friends.
- What kind of things do you talk about with your friends?
- What influence have your family and friends had on you?
- What interests do your family and friends have?

Money and possessions

- What would you buy if you suddenly had a lot of money? ..... (Why?)
- Do you want to be richer than you are now? ..... (Why? / Why not?)
- What do people of your age generally want to buy? ..... (Why?)
- What are your favourite possessions? ..... (Why?)
- What would you like to own in the future? ..... (Why?)

TEST 2

1   Films
2   Cooking

Candidate A	Look at the two photographs 1A and 1B on page 123. They show adverts for films.
	Compare the photographs and say what the characteristics of each kind of film are.
	Candidate A talks on his / her own for about 1 minute.
Candidate B	Which of the films would you prefer to see, and why?
	Candidate B talks on his / her own for about 20 seconds.
Candidate B	Look at the two photographs 2A and 2B on page 123. They show people cooking meals.
	Compare the photographs and say what you think the situation is in each photograph.
	Candidate B talks on his / her own for about 1 minute.
Candidate A	Which of the people cooking would you prefer to be, and why?
	Candidate A talks on his / her own for about 20 seconds.

TEST 2

'Special day' prize

PART 3

Imagine that you are organizing a competition at the place where you work or study. The prize for the winner is going to be a special day and you have to choose what kind of special day the prize will be. Look at the special days offered by a company in their brochure on page 124.

First, talk to each other about how attractive each of the possible prizes would be. Then decide which one should be the prize.

Candidates A and B discuss this together for about 3 minutes.

PART 4

- Which of the special days would you like to experience personally? ..... (Why?)
- Which of the special days would you definitely not want to take part in? ...... (Why?)
- What dangerous sports are popular in your country?
- What makes people want to take part in dangerous sports?
- Why do people like going to theme parks? Which ones are good and which ones are not, in your opinion?
- Some people say that young people don't have a wide range of interests. Do you agree?

Paper 1: Reading (1 hour)

You are going to read a newspaper article about careers advice. For questions 1–8, choose the answer (A, B, C or D) which you think fits best according to the text.

Mark your answers on the separate answer sheet.

Finding the career that fits your personality

'If you've finished your exams and have absolutely no idea what to do next, you're not alone,' says Sheridan Hughes, an occupational psychologist at Career Analysts, a career counselling service. 'At 18, it can be very difficult to know what you want to do because you don't really know what you're interested in.' Careers guidance, adds Alexis Hallam, one of her colleagues, is generally poor and 'people can end up in the wrong job and stay there for years because they're good at something without actually enjoying it.'

To discover what people are good at, and more fundamentally, what they will enjoy doing, Career Analysts give their clients a battery of personality profile questionnaires and psychometric tests. An in-depth interview follows, in which the test results are discussed and different career paths and options are explored with the aid of an occupational psychologist. Career Analysts offers guidance to everyone, from teenagers to retirees looking for a new focus in life. The service sounded just what I needed. Dividing my time as I do between teaching and freelance journalism, I definitely need advice about consolidating my career. Being too ancient for Career Analysts' student career option guidance and not, unfortunately, at the executive level yet, I opted for the career management package. This is aimed at people who are established in their jobs and who either want a change or some advice about planning the next step in their careers.

Having filled in a multitude of personality indicator questionnaires at home, I then spent a rather gruelling morning being aptitude-tested at Career Analysts' offices. The tests consisted of logical reasoning followed by verbal, mechanical and spatial aptitude papers. Logical reasoning required me to pick out the next shape in a sequence of triangles, squares and oblongs. I tried my best but knew that it was really a lost cause. I fared rather better when it came to verbal aptitude - finding the odd one out in a series of words couldn't be simpler. My complacency was short-lived, however, when I was confronted with images of levers and pulleys for the mechanical aptitude papers. My mind went blank. I had no idea what would happen to wheel X when string Y was pulled.

At home, filling in questionnaires, I had been asked to give my instinctive reaction (not an over-considered one) to statements like: 'It bothers me if people think I'm being odd or unconventional', or 'I like to do my planning alone without interruptions from others.' I was asked to agree or disagree on a scale of one to five with 'I often take on impossible odds', or 'It is impossible for me to believe that chance or luck plays an important role in my life.' I was told to indicate how important I consider status to be in a job, and how important money and material benefits.

The questions attempt to construct a picture of the complete individual. Using aptitude tests alongside personality profiling, occupational psychologists will, the theory goes, be able to guide a client towards a rewarding, fulfilling career. Some questions are as straightforward as indicating whether or not you would enjoy a particular job. Designing aircraft runways? Preparing legal documents? Playing a musical instrument? Every career going makes an appearance and, as I was shown later, the responses tend to form a coherent pattern.

Having completed my personality and aptitude tests, I sat down with Sheridan Hughes, who asked me fairly searching personal and professional questions. What do my parents and siblings do for a living? Why had I chosen to do an English degree? 'I need to get a picture of you as a person and how you've come to be who you are,' she explained. 'What we do works because it's a mixture of science and counselling. We use objective psychometric measures to discover our clients' natural strengths and abilities and then we talk to them about what they want from life.'

There were no real surprises in my own test results, nor in the interview that followed it. 'We're interested in patterns,' Mrs Hughes explained, 'and the pattern for you is strongly verbal and communicative.' This was putting it rather kindly. I had come out as average on the verbal skills test and below average in logic, numerical, perceptual and mechanical reasoning. My spatial visualization was so bad it was almost off the scale. 'A career in cartography, navigation, tiling or architecture would not be playing to your strengths,' she said delicately.

Mrs Hughes encouraged me to expand the writing side of my career and gave me straightforward, practical suggestions as to how I could go about it. 'Widen the scope of your articles,' she said. 'You could develop an interest in medical and psychological fields.' These latter, she said, would sit comfortably with an interest in human behaviour indicated on my personality-profiling questionnaires. She suggested that I consider writing e-learning content for on-line courses, an avenue that would never have occurred to me.

1 Which of the following is mentioned in the first paragraph?

    A people underestimating their own abilities
    B people accepting inappropriate advice
    C people being unwilling to take risks
    D people constantly changing their minds

1

2 What does the writer say about Career Analysts in the second paragraph?

    A It is about to offer a service for people at executive level.
    B The range of services it offers is unique.
    C She was initially doubtful that it could be useful to her.
    D Only one of its services was relevant to her.

2

3 What happened when the writer took the aptitude tests?

    A She found two of the papers extremely difficult.
    B She put in very little effort on any of them.
    C She didn't understand what she was required to do on one of them.
    D The papers were not what she had been expecting.

3

4 What does the writer say about the statements on the questionnaires?

    A She thought about them for longer than she was supposed to.
    B She found some of them rather strange.
    C One of them focused on her attitude to risk.
    D One of them concerned her current situation only.

4

5 The writer says that the idea behind the questionnaires is that

    A people will find some of the questions quite hard to answer.
    B the answers to them and the aptitude tests will provide all the
       necessary information.
    C they will encourage people to have new ideas about possible careers.
    D they will give a more accurate picture of people than the aptitude tests.

5

6 Some of the questions Sheridan Hughes asked concerned the writer's

    A opinions of the tests and questionnaires.
    B relationships with family members.
    C main regrets.
    D progress through life.

6

7 The writer felt that during the interview, Mrs Hughes

    A was keen not to upset her concerning her test results.
    B seemed surprised at how badly she had done in the tests.
    C was being honest about her strengths and weaknesses.
    D preferred to avoid talking about her test results.

7

8 The advice Mrs Hughes gave to the writer included the suggestion that she should

    A think about taking a course on writing.
    B concentrate only on writing and not on any other kind of work.
    C increase the number of subjects she writes about.
    D do something she had previously considered unappealing.

8

TEST 3

You are going to read an article about martial arts. Seven sentences have been removed from the article. Choose from the sentences A–H the one which fits each gap (9–15). There is one extra sentence which you do not need to use.

Mark your answers on the separate answer sheet.

Martial Arts Classes

Learn an effective fighting and self-defence system

Tony Chang is a martial artist who has served a long apprenticeship in both the internal and external arts. He is respected worldwide as a martial arts instructor in kenpo, t'ai chi ch'uan and chi kung and runs several of his own clubs in Manchester. He also has several training videos and DVDs to his credit. In fact, he was one of the pioneers of teaching the Martial Arts Techniques series on the worldwide web. **9** _____

Tony is now in the process of producing what he considers to be the 'ultimate street survival' DVD, combining fighting and self-defence with energy (chi) development and enhancement. A few years ago, he was inducted into the Martial Arts Hall of Fame for integrating his internal martial arts knowledge with the fast-paced external striking style that kenpo is noted for, and developing kenpo taiji. **10** _____

It is not based purely on physical strength. **11** _____ As Tony explains, 'It is 50 per cent physical and 50 per cent in the mind. It is a scientific fact that we have three brains inside our head. As well as the intellectual brain which forms 90 per cent of our overall brain, five per cent is the artistic brain which is responsible for subconscious body movement and five per cent constitutes the reptilian brain, which is purely reflex. This is the same brain as that of all reptiles, such as snakes and crocodiles – this is our survival brain.'

12 _____ That is because they use the logical, intellectual brain to teach logical pre-arranged techniques. However, fighting is totally illogical and we cannot apply logic to an illogical situation, so our response to an attack must be reflex. Students achieve this in kenpo taiji by learning how to access their reptilian brain. Tony says there is no time to think in a fight situation. 'If you stop to think, you'll get hit,' he explains.

Tony is running beginners' classes in kenpo taiji. **13** _____ These include how to adopt certain body postures which encourage energy to flow from an energy storage centre known as the *dan tien* up to the brain stem. Students are then in reptile brain mode, ready to defend themselves against any attacker. And they learn training methods designed by the ancient Chinese masters to programme this part of the brain subconsciously with correct fighting principles.

In addition to using the subconscious brain, kenpo taiji also applies the principle of *dim mak*, or pressure point fighting. Perfect health is dependent on a healthy flow of chi through the body's meridians and students learn to disrupt the flow of chi by striking dim mak (acupuncture) points along these meridians. **14** _____ This is because they are using energy disruption rather than purely physical strength.

As well as being an effective fighting and self-defence system, kenpo taiji teaches students to develop and intensify the flow of their own internal energy (chi) by training in chi kung and traditional t'ai chi ch'uan, enabling them to achieve perfect health. **15** _____ And in addition to that, during the classes some of the greatest martial arts secrets are revealed by Tony.

A By doing this, they are able to respond to an attack with relative ease.

B If that were the case, the stronger, bigger person would always win.

C As a result of such experiences, more and more people are taking it up.

D This is one of the most formidable street survival, fighting and self-defence systems ever invented.

E Students attending these are taught several training methods.

F If you take it up, you will learn how to get into this condition and you will be able to defend yourself whatever your size, age or gender.

G Many others have now followed his lead.

H Most martial arts are not street effective.

PART 3

You are going to read a magazine article about the best way to see certain artistic masterpieces in various buildings. For questions 16–30, choose from the buildings (A–F). The buildings may be chosen more than once.

Mark your answers on the separate answer sheet.

Of which building are the following stated?

Different categories of visitor are anxious to view the masterpiece.	16
Some people have the wrong idea about when the building is open.	17
You may have some difficulty making your arrangements for your visit.	18
There are plenty of excellent works of art in the building that do not attract many viewers.	19
On your return journey through the building, you can look at works of art you missed earlier.	20
People who work there make a big claim about the masterpiece.	21
You will be able to get to the masterpiece before other visitors, because they will stop to view other works of art.	22
Holidaymakers do not normally visit the building but it is an excellent place.	23
There is another work of art in the building apart from the masterpiece that is equally worth seeing.	24
A rule prevents people from viewing the masterpiece for too long.	25
The masterpiece has not always received the praise it currently receives.	26
It is possible that visitor numbers to the museum will increase.	27
Make sure you remain in front of the crowds of people as you go through the building.	28
There is a period when most visitors have left the building.	29
One suggestion for visiting the building is not as unrealistic as it may appear.	30

Smart Art

The queue-buster's guide to the world's greatest masterpieces

Early openings, private viewings –
here's everything you need for a magic
moment with the world's most famous
masterpieces

A The Birth of Venus

Uffizi, Florence, Italy

The Florentine master Sandro Botticelli
created one of the most graceful and
joyful images of the modern age, and
the single most popular painting in the
Uffizi. To see it at its best, you need
to pre-book a ticket for timed entry
at 8.15 a.m., courtesy of the Firenze
Musei booking service; don't be put off
if you can't get through on the phone
first time. Once inside, head straight
for the suite of rooms 10-14, where the
Botticellis are displayed. Then take in
the other highlights of the collection –
the Da Vincis in room 15, the Raphaels
in room 26, and the Caravaggios in
room 43 – staying ahead of the hordes
as you go. If there are any gaps you want
to fill in, work backwards towards the
entrance: by now, the crowds will be
unavoidable, but you'll have already had
the masters to yourself.

B The Death Mask of Tutankhamun

Egyptian Museum, Cairo, Egypt

It is, of course, impossible for one object
to embody the vigour and sophistication
of ancient Egypt's culture. But
the funerary mask of the boy-king
Tutankhamun comes close. Eleven kilos
of solid gold, inlaid with lapis lazuli,
glass paste and semi-precious stones,
it's the undisputed star of the Egyptian
Museum – which, given the array of
mummies, colossi, thrones and jewellery
on show here, gives you an idea of its
charisma. Whatever the season, there
are people clamouring to see it: hefty
groups from the cruise liners and Red
Sea resorts in the summer and a steady
stream of culture-vultures on Nile
tours in the cooler months. At least
the museum's policy of not allowing
guides to talk in front of its display case,
in room 3 up on the first floor, means
that the flow of visitors doesn't get too

congested. But if you want some proper
quiet, you need to come at lunchtime.
There are fewer independent travellers
about, and it's changeover time for
the tour parties too. The quietest time
is between 11.30 a.m. and 2 p.m. on
midweek days in July and August, when
the bus tours take all the tourists away
for their lunches.

C The Sistine Ceiling

Vatican Museums, Rome, Italy

The really smart way to see
Michelangelo's masterwork is on a
private tour. At first sight, this looks
prohibitively expensive. But form
a group of like-minded friends, and
suddenly you have the experience of an
art-loving lifetime for the price of dinner
for two in a posh restaurant. If that's
not an option, then you've got to be first
in, which means arriving at the vast
Vatican Museums complex at least an
hour before the doors open, armed with
a good map (most Rome guidebooks
have them) and a pair of binoculars.
Once you're inside, hurry to the chapel
– it's at the far end of the complex, and
most people will be distracted by some
of the other world-class exhibits. The
binoculars, by the way, are essential.

Michelangelo's forms hover some 20m
overhead.

D Girl With A Pearl Earring

*Mauritshuis, The Hague,
The Netherlands*

Vermeer's delicate, deeply ambiguous
portrait is one of the most finely
observed in all western art. Its home,
the Mauristshuis, is some way off the
tourist map – even though it's one of
the best small museums in Europe – but
Dutch school kids make the pilgrimage
in droves. A Monday in summer is your
best bet for a private view – it's closed
that day in winter, and locals assume
it's a year-round day off.

E The Kiss

Belvedere, Vienna, Austria

Vienna may now be second only to Paris
as art-history capital of Europe, but
city-breakers have yet to realize this fact,
and many of its wonderful exhibits are
mercifully uncrowded. Klimt's ravishing
Kiss, beloved of student bedrooms, does
draw a devoted following, though. Go
in the early morning, or on Thursday
evening, to be sure of the best viewing
conditions. While you're there, don't
miss Klimt's other great painting, his
1907 portrait of Adele Bloch-Bauer.
It's as dazzling and sensual in effect
as *The Kiss*.

F Les Demoiselles d'Avignon

Museum of Modern Art, New York, US

Picasso's confrontational and
revolutionary painting was by no means
considered a masterpiece when he
showed it to his friends in 1907. Matisse
laughed out loud when he first saw it.
Others were stunned into embarrassed
silence. There's no doubting its value
now: the Museum of Modern Art's
curators call it 'perhaps the single
most influential work in the history of
modern art'. Few would argue. Your best
strategy for a crowd-free view is to join a
private group before the doors open. If
you don't want to do that, book a timed-
entry ticket for 10.30 a.m. Gallery 2, on
the fourth floor, is your goal.

Paper 2: Writing (1 hour 20 minutes)

PART 1

*You **must** answer this question. Write your answer in 120–150 words in an appropriate style.*

1 You have received a letter replying to a letter of complaint that you wrote to a shop manager. Read the letter you received and the notes you have made. Then write another letter to the manager, using **all** your notes.

Holt Electronics
Grange Retail Park
Birmingham B5 6TY

Dear Customer,

he was rude

I am sorry that you found the level of service in our shop unsatisfactory when you came in to have the computer you had bought from us repaired. The assistant you spoke to tells me that he did his best to help but was unable to carry out the repairs while you waited. We do point out in our service guarantee that repairs may take several days, depending on the nature of the problem.

it says 'speedy repairs'

We are proud of the quality of the products that we sell, and have a high level of customer satisfaction with them. I hope that you do not have any further problems with your computer and that you will continue to shop with us.

mine keeps going wrong

no chance!

Yours sincerely,

Fiona Baker
Branch Manager

Write your **letter**. You must use grammatically correct sentences with accurate spelling and punctuation in a style appropriate for the situation.

PART 2

Write an answer to one of the questions 2–5 in this part. Write your answer in 120–180 words in an appropriate style.

2   Your teacher has asked you to write a story for an international magazine. The story must **begin** with the following words:

> When I started on the journey, I had no idea what was going to happen.

Write your **story**.

3   You have seen this announcement in an international magazine.

> **MY FAVOURITE HOBBY**
>
> What's your passion when you're not working or studying? Tell us all about it and why you like it. What does it involve? What made you take it up and how much of your time do you spend on it?
>
> We'll publish the best articles in a special section next month.

Write your **article**.

4   You recently saw this notice in an international magazine.

> **WHAT ARE THE LATEST FASHIONS WHERE YOU ARE?**
>
> We're looking for people to send us reports on the latest fashions among young people in the places where they live. You can tell us about fashions in music, in clothes, in what people buy, in behaviour or anything else you want to describe. And give your opinions on these fashions too. We'll publish some of the reports so that our readers can compare fashions in different places.

Write your **report**.

5   Answer **one** of the following two questions based on your reading of **one** of the set books.

Either

5(a) Write a **letter** to a friend about the book, explaining what you thought of it and saying why you think that your friend would enjoy reading it.

Or

5(b) Write an **essay** comparing the book with another book that you have read. In what ways are the two books different and in what ways are they similar? In what ways is one of the books better than the other?

Paper 3: Use of English (45 minutes)

<u>PART 1</u>

For questions 1–12, read the text below and decide which answer (A, B, C or D) best fits each gap. There is an example at the beginning (0).

Mark your answers on the separate answer sheet.

Example:

0   **A** convince   **B** guess   **C** believe   **D** value

0	A	B	C	D

Neighbours influence buying decisions

However objective we **0**_____ ourselves to be, most of us do not judge a product solely on its merits, considering quality, value and style before making a decision. **1**_____ , we are easily influenced by the people around us.

There is nothing **2**_____ with this. It is probably a smarter way to make decisions than **3**_____ on only our own opinions. But it does make life hard for companies. They have **4**_____ understood that groups of friends and relatives tend to buy the same products, but understanding the reasons has been tricky. Is it because they are so similar with **5**_____ to how much money they make and what television ads they watch that they independently **6**_____ at the same decision? Or do they copy one another, perhaps **7**_____ envy or perhaps because they have shared information about the products?

Research in Finland recently found overwhelming evidence that neighbours have a big influence on buying decisions. When one of a person's ten nearest neighbours bought a car, the **8**_____ that that person would buy a car of the same brand during the next week and a half **9**_____ by 86 per cent. The researchers argued that it was not just a **10**_____ of envy. Used cars seemed to attract neighbours even more than new cars. This suggested that people were not trying to **11**_____ up with their neighbours, they were keen to learn from them. Since used cars are less reliable, a recommendation of one can **12**_____ influence a buying decision.

1	**A** What's more	**B** Instead	**C** Unlike	**D** In place
2	**A** wrong	**B** silly	**C** bad	**D** daft
3	**A** basing	**B** trusting	**C** supposing	**D** relying
4	**A** ever	**B** far	**C** much	**D** long
5	**A** connection	**B** regard	**C** relation	**D** concern
6	**A** reach	**B** come	**C** arrive	**D** get
7	**A** for	**B** as to	**C** out of	**D** about
8	**A** chances	**B** potential	**C** possibilities	**D** forecast
9	**A** boosted	**B** rose	**C** enlarged	**D** lifted
10	**A** thing	**B** point	**C** matter	**D** fact
11	**A** keep	**B** stay	**C** hold	**D** follow
12	**A** fiercely	**B** strongly	**C** firmly	**D** intensely

*For questions 13–24, read the text below and think of the word which best fits each gap. Use only **one** word in each gap. There is an example at the beginning (0).*

Write your answers IN CAPITAL LETTERS on the separate answer sheet.

Example:

| 0 | S | O | M | E | T | H | I | N | G | | | | |

Learning a musical instrument

Learning to play an instrument is **0** _SOMETHING_ that can give a lot of pleasure. It's also an achievement and a skill **13** _____ stays with you for life. Music has a part to play in everyone's life, and has been described **14** _____ a 'primary language'.

Learning to play an instrument isn't easy at the beginning **15** _____ takes effort and determination. And while there's nothing wrong with aiming **16** _____ the top, music is definitely **17** _____ something to take up because you think you ought **18** _____ do it.

A lot of adults regret not **19** _____ learnt to play an instrument when they were younger. But it is never **20** _____ late to learn! And the advantages of learning an instrument are far greater than just the pleasure of producing a marvellous sound. When you've progressed far **21** _____, there are lots of amateur groups which you can join **22** _____ you want to be part of a larger group. Once you've reached a good enough standard to join a band or orchestra, you add the team skills like **23** _____ you get from playing sport. There's also a great social side to playing with others, as **24** _____ as the chance to travel through touring.

PART 3

For questions 25–34, read the text below. Use the word given in capitals at the end of some of the lines to form a word that fits in the gap in the same line. There is an example at the beginning (0).

Write your answers IN CAPITAL LETTERS *on the separate answer sheet.*

Example:

0	F	R	I	E	N	D	L	Y					

THE COUPLES WITH IDENTICAL LIVES

When Frank and Vera Jackson met a 0 _____ couple on holiday | FRIEND

in Spain also called Frank and Vera (but with a different

surname: Bentley), at first they must have laughed at the 25 _____ . | COINCIDE

But when they got into 26 _____ with their namesakes, they made | CONVERSE

some surprising 27 _____ and realized that they had much more in | DISCOVER

common.

    The two couples, both in their 28 _____ and from the UK, had booked | SEVENTY

their trips to Barcelona at the same time. This was not so 29 _____ . | LIKELY

However, both couples had had their 30 _____ at 3 p.m. on July 26th, | WED

1951. Both couples each had two daughters, with dates of 31 _____ | BORN

in 1952 and 1956, and six grandchildren. Mr Jackson worked in the car

industry in Oxford; Mr Bentley did 32 _____ the same job but in | EXACT

Dagenham. Their wives, who had both worked for the same bank, had both

lost their 33 _____ rings and were wearing identical gold watches. | ENGAGE

'I'm sure people everywhere lead identical lives,' said Mr Jackson, 'but to

meet our doubles was 34 _____ .' | BELIEVE

For questions 35–42, complete the second sentence so that it has a similar meaning to the first sentence, using the word given. Do not change the word given. *You must use between* two *and* five *words, including the word given. Here is an example (0).*

Example:

0   Making new friends was easy for her.

   DIFFICULT

   She didn't _____ new friends.

The gap can be filled with the words 'find it difficult to make', so you write:

| 0 | F | I | N | D | | I | T | | D | I | F | F | I | C | U | L | T | | T | O | | M | A | K | E | | |

Write the missing words IN CAPITAL LETTERS *on the separate answer sheet.*

---

35   Because of what you advised me, I did the right thing.

   ADVICE

   Thanks _____ me, I did the right thing.

36   In my opinion, they're the best band in the world.

   CONCERNED

   They're the best band in the world, as _____

37   Her behaviour tends to be bad when she is under pressure.

   TENDENCY

   She _____ badly when she is under pressure.

38   My brother earns half of what I earn.

   TWICE

   I earn _____ my brother.

39   I got angry because of the assistant's attitude.

   MADE

   The assistant's attitude _____ temper.

40   He plays so skilfully that nobody can beat him.

   MUCH

   He plays with _____ that nobody can beat him.

41   They were late because they got stuck in traffic.

   RESULT

   They were late _____ stuck in traffic.

42   Yesterday I met one of my friends by chance in the supermarket.

   RAN

   Yesterday I _____ mine in the supermarket.

Paper 4: Listening (40 minutes)

<u>PART 1</u>

You will hear people talking in eight different situations. For questions 1–8, choose the best answer, (A, B or C).

1   You hear part of an interview with a pop singer.
    How does she feel about what happened?

    A   embarrassed by her mistake

    B   angry with her tour manager | 1 |

    C   confused about what happened

2   You hear part of a radio programme for young people.
    What advice does the speaker give?

    A   Try to discuss the matter with your friends.

    B   Pay no attention to the people who laugh at you. | 2 |

    C   Encourage other people to be like you.

3   You hear a radio presenter talking about a book.
    What does the presenter say about the book?

    A   Some of the writers have already had their work published.

    B   It contains work that was entered for a competition. | 3 |

    C   It is very well organized.

4   You hear someone talking on the phone.
    What is the speaker's purpose?

    A   to resolve a disagreement

    B   to make a threat | 4 |

    C   to apologize for previous behaviour

5   You hear someone talking to an assistant at a box office.
    What is the situation?

    A   The man has lost his tickets.

    B   The man was sent the wrong tickets.   5

    C   The man wants to return the tickets.

6   You hear someone talking about her personality.
    What is the speaker doing?

    A   admitting something

    B   explaining something   6

    C   promising something

7   You hear two people talking.
    What is the relationship between them?

    A   They are members of the same club.

    B   They live in the same building.   7

    C   They are studying on the same course.

8   You hear a local radio presenter talking about a competition.
    Which of the following is true of the competition?

    A   The first part does not involve any cooking.

    B   The second part involves ten people cooking on their own. 8

    C   The final part takes place at a different restaurant.

PART 2

You will hear an interview with a representative of a wildlife park called Paradise Wildlife Park. For questions 9–18, complete the sentences.

PARADISE WILDLIFE PARK

Project Life Lion is connected with diseases spread by [_____ 9] in Africa.

The Park has created its own [_____ 10] system, and other organizations use it.

A wide variety of [_____ 11] events (e.g. barbecues) are held at the Park.

For charity events, the Park will provide cheap tickets and [_____ 12].

The Park's sister company gives people a chance to be a [_____ 13].

People paying to adopt an animal get a [_____ 14], a photograph, information about the animal and a free ticket for two people.

People who visit the Park [_____ 15] in a year benefit from having a season ticket.

When the weather is cold, visitors can still enjoy using the [_____ 16].

One of the Experience Days involves being an [_____ 17] for a day.

The Park is looking for people to do customer service and [_____ 18] work.

You will hear five different people talking about what they discovered when they read autobiographies by famous people. For questions 19–23, choose from the list (A–F) what each person says that they discovered. Use the letters only once. There is one extra letter which you do not need to use.

A   He had a terrible life before becoming famous.

Speaker 1	19

B   He is a nicer person than he appears to be.

Speaker 2	20

C   He is exactly the same in private as he is in public.

Speaker 3	21

D   He would have preferred a different career.

Speaker 4	22

E   He was very unkind to other people after he became famous.

Speaker 5	23

F   He feels that he is a very important person.

TEST 3

PART 4

You will hear an interview with someone whose daughters are appearing in a show in London. For questions 24–30, choose the best answer (A, B or C).

24 What does Jackie say about Olivia's role in *Annie*?

    A Olivia had difficulty learning such a big role.

    B Olivia had always wanted to have such a big role.

    C Olivia hadn't expected to get such a big role.

    24

25 Jackie says that Olivia's performance in *Annie*

    A did not surprise other members of her family.

    B was helped by advice from an agent.

    C contrasted with her normal personality.

    25

26 When Olivia tried to get a part in *Mary Poppins*, she

    A did not really expect to get the part.

    B was extremely upset not to get the part.

    C was immediately rejected for the part.

    26

27 What happened at the first auditions for *The Sound of Music*?

    A Jackie's children were told they would have to come back the next day.

    B The family arrived later than they had been told to arrive.

    C There were so many people that the family considered leaving.

    27

28 For the second audition, both girls

    A decided to wear similar clothes.

    B were required to sing two songs.

    C felt they had to improve.

    28

29 At the final audition,

    A neither of the girls appeared to be nervous.

    B Jackie told them they looked right for the parts.

    C both girls made jokes about the event.

    29

30 How have the girls reacted to getting the parts?

    A They are a bit concerned that their lives will change.

    B The achievement has made them more self-confident.

    C Their behaviour has remained the same as it was before.

    30

TEST 3

Paper 5: Speaking (14 minutes)

<u>PART 1</u> (3 minutes)

Sport

- What's your favourite sport? ..... (Why?)
- Which sport(s) do you dislike? ..... (Why?)
- Which sports are popular in your country?
- Do you support a particular team? Is it a successful team?
- What is your experience of taking part in sports?

The news

- Do you take an interest in what's happening in the news? ..... (Why? / Why not?)
- What newspaper(s) do you read? Describe it / them.
- What is the news on TV like in your country?
- Apart from newspapers and TV, what other sources of news can you use?
- What's your opinion of the way the media present the news?

PART 2 (4 minutes)

    1   Taking photographs
    2   At the airport

Candidate A	Look at the two photographs 1A and 1B on page 125. They show people taking photographs.
	Compare the photographs and say why the person is taking the photograph.
	Candidate A talks on his / her own for about 1 minute.
Candidate B	Which of the photographs being taken do you prefer, and why?
	Candidate B talks on his / her own for about 20 seconds.
Candidate B	Look at the two photographs 2A and 2B on page 125. They show people at airports.
	Compare the photographs and say what the situation is in each one.
	Candidate B talks on his / her own for about 1 minute.
Candidate A	Which of the people would you prefer to be, and why?
	Candidate A talks on his / her own for about 20 seconds.

Planning a festival

PART 3

Imagine that you are responsible for planning a one-day festival that will take place on a local field. Look at the plan of the field and at the possible things to include in the festival on page 126.

First, talk to each other about which things to include in the festival. Then decide where each of them should be.

Candidates A and B discuss this together for about 3 minutes.

PART 4

- What kind of local events take place where you come from? Do young people take part in or attend them?
- Would you like to organize an event like this? ..... (Why? / Why not?)
- What's the best event you've ever attended? Why was it so good?
- What's the worst event you've ever attended? Why was it so bad?
- Do you think that local life is changing where you come from? ..... (Why / Why not?)
- Some people think that in the modern world, local communities are not as important as they used to be. Do you agree?

TEST 3

Paper 1: Reading (1 hour)

You are going to read a newspaper article about holidays. For questions 1–8, choose the answer (A, B, C or D) which you think fits best according to the text.

Mark your answers on the separate answer sheet.

Why I've taken a break from holidays

It's a wonderful morning, as I write this: hot, but without being too hot. Outside my window, I can see the bluest, sunniest sky of the year reflected in a huge natural expanse of water. It's the kind of sun that makes you acutely aware of summer's temporary nature - a reminder that if I am ever going to get around to booking this year's holiday, time is running out. For a moment, the idea of sitting on a beach in a place where this kind of weather is nothing remarkable, catching up on my reading, sounds tempting, but then a tension begins to rise in my chest and the temptation passes.

It is now close to four years since I last took a holiday. This is because I have come to the conclusion, over the course of my adult life, that I am not very good at it. You might think this sounds like saying you're not very good at drinking tea or listening to music. What could possibly be difficult about the natural act of putting your working life on hold for a couple of weeks and going somewhere warm to do nothing?

To be honest, I'm a little baffled myself. I was a model holidaymaker as a kid: every July, I would arrive at an Italian campsite with my parents and, within a couple of days, my skin would have turned an olive colour and I would blend into my surroundings so totally that I would often find myself being mistakenly told to join a party of local schoolchildren. The problems started during my early twenties: a stolen tent and wallet at the Glastonbury Festival in 1995; a lightning strike and sudden drop in altitude on a flight over the Channel in 1997; an ill-fated experiment in 'luxury inter-railing' in 1998 that lasted just four days and ended with the French police mistaking me for a drug smuggler.

But even if I manage to go away without being mugged or getting food poisoning, I now find that I can't really commit to the experience. A fancy-free trip to the South of France five years ago to 'just kind of hang out on the coast' was ended after just two days, mainly because I had an urge to check my e-mails. Similarly, my honeymoon, a year or so later, was cut short by 48 hours – not because my wife and I weren't enjoying ourselves, but because we were missing our cats.

So what is my problem? On the surface, I'm probably a bit of a homebody. And I just find the pressure of being on holiday too severe: it always feels like having a gun held to my head and being forced to have fun. Somehow, packing a carefully itemised list of possessions and meeting a scheduled flight has none of the excitement of suddenly deciding to take a day off and driving somewhere for the fun of it.

Thankfully, I'm not alone. This summer, most of my friends have decided not to have a break. And a recent survey highlighted the downside of holidays, with the results showing that nearly two thirds of people found that the calming effects of a holiday wore off within 24 hours, as stress levels returned to normal. And this year *The Idler* magazine published its *Book of Awful Holidays*. Here you will find a list of the five most ecologically-damaging vacations it's possible to take, along with 50 horrific holiday experiences voted for on *The Idler* website. Over the last decade, *The Idler* has become well known for promoting the idea of an easy, lazy life. The leisure industry might seem an unlikely target of its criticism, but Dan Kiernan, the book's editor, says that he was flooded with entries from readers for his list of Awful Holidays.

'What interests me is what the concept of a "holiday" says about the rest of our lives,' he explains. 'We all seem content to slave away for 48 weeks a year and only get four off. For me, the point of living is to have a life you enjoy for 52 weeks a year.' He has a point. The more I like my life and the better I structure it, the less I want to go away. Maybe I'm weird for not liking holidays, but I just feel my leisure time is too valuable to waste on them.

1 The writer says in the first paragraph that while he is writing this article,

   A he feels envious of people who are on holiday.
   B he realizes it is too late to book a holiday.
   C he wishes that the weather would change.
   D he experiences a brief desire to book a holiday.

1

2 What does the writer suggest about the fact that he has not taken a holiday for four years?

   A Some people may find the reason surprising.
   B He often has to explain the reason to other people.
   C There have been times when he has regretted it.
   D It is not something he has thought about before.

2

3 What is the writer describing in the third paragraph?

   A events that explain why he has never really liked holidays
   B events that he regards as not typical of most people's experiences
   C events that illustrate his contrasting experiences of holidays
   D events that he did not consider particularly serious when they happened

3

4 The events the writer describes in the fourth paragraph illustrate

   A how hard he has tried to enjoy holidays.
   B how badly he behaves when he is on holiday.
   C his fear that something bad will happen when he is on holiday.
   D his lack of enthusiasm for being on holiday.

4

5 The writer says in the fifth paragraph that the main thing he dislikes about holidays is that

   A they are often organized in order to please other people.
   B they are far less enjoyable than breaks that have not been planned in advance.
   C he tends to be made responsible for too much of the organization of them.
   D he feels embarrassed when other people are having fun but he isn't.

5

6 The writer says that a recent survey shows that a lot of people

   A pretend to enjoy their holidays.
   B fail to relax while they are on holiday.
   C feel that the benefits of going on holiday are limited.
   D have made the same decision as the writer and most of his friends.

6

7 The writer says that the book published by *The Idler* magazine

   A illustrates a point that the magazine has often made.
   B proved more popular than he would have expected.
   C focuses entirely on bad personal experiences of holidays.
   D indicates that his dislike of holidays is widely shared.

7

8 When the writer says 'He has a point' in the final paragraph, he is agreeing that

   A people who like their normal lives don't need to go on holiday.
   B some people need to have holidays but others don't.
   C not liking holidays is generally considered strange.
   D a lot of people don't really want to go on holiday.

8

You are going to read an article about maps showing the homes of film stars. Seven sentences have been removed from the article. Choose from the sentences A–H the one which fits each gap (9–15). There is one extra sentence which you do not need to use.

Mark your answers on the separate answer sheet.

Maps of the stars

Ever since the 1910s, when film-makers like Cecil B. DeMille first set up shop in Hollywood, mapmakers, the explorers of the city's social terrain, have been compiling that only-in-Los Angeles fixture, maps showing the locations of the fabulous homes of the stars. Collectively, they form an unofficial version of the Oscars, reflecting who's in and who's out in the film world. 'Each one looks different,' says Linda Welton, whose grandfather and mother pioneered these maps. **9** _____ Former icons vanish from them, new ones appear on them, and some of the truly greats are permanent fixtures on them.

In 1933, noticing the steady stream of tourists drifting westward to follow the stars from Hollywood to Beverly Hills, the nearby district where most of the stars went to live, Ms Welton's grandfather, Wesley G Lake, obtained a copyright for his *Guide to Starland Estates and Mansions.* **10** _____ For 40 years Ms Welton's mother, Vivienne E Welton, sold maps just down the road from Gary Cooper's place at 200 Baroda*. The asterisk indicates that it was the actor's final home, as opposed to a plus sign (denoting a former home) or a zero (for no view from the street).

'My grandfather asked Mom to talk to the gardeners to find out where the stars lived,' Ms Welton recalls. 'She'd say: "Oh, this is a beautiful garden. Who lives here?" Who would suspect a little girl?' Ms Welton and her crew now sell about 10,000 maps a year from a folding chair parked curbside six days a week. **11** _____

The evolution of the maps mirrors both the Hollywood publicity machine and real estate and tourism development. **12** _____ The first celebrity home, according to Marc Wanamaker, a historian and a founder of the Westwood and Beverly Hills Historical Societies, belonged to the artist Paul de Longpre. He had a luxuriously-landscaped house at Cahuenga Avenue and Hollywood and real estate agents would take prospective clients past it on tours.

Although it is not known for certain who published the first map, by the mid-1920s all sorts of people were producing them. **13** _____

One of the most famous of the early maps was produced to show the location of Pickfair, the sprawling home of the newly married stars Mary Pickford and Douglas Fairbanks Sr, and the homes of some of their star friends. During World War I, they opened their home to serve refreshments to soldiers. As Vivienne Welton once explained in an interview with *Mercator's World*, a map and cartography magazine, 'She urged a few friends to do the same. **14** _____'

For over 40 years, people have marched toward the corner of Sunset and Baroda with hand-painted yellow signs saying: 'Star Maps, 2 blocks', 'Star Maps, 1 block', 'Star Maps here'. The maps reflect the shifting geography of stardom as celebrities, seeking escape from over-enthusiastic fans, some with ill intentions, have moved out to Pacific Palisades or the Pacific Coast Highway in Malibu. **15** _____ Legendary stars – Garbo, Monroe, Chaplin – remain on them. Others, however, hang on for about a decade and then vanish.

A   As they do so, they give advice to the tourists on star safaris through the lime green landscape of Beverly Hills.

B   Studios like Paramount published the names and addresses of its stars on theirs, and businesses distributed them as a promotional gimmick.

C   Others, however, say that the star maps are still an essential part of Hollywood and the film world.

D   More profoundly, perhaps, the maps suggest the temporary nature of fame.

E   Early film stars like Lillian Gish lived in modest, somewhat grubby rooming houses, taking street cars to and from the studio.

F   Updated regularly, they are still for sale at the corner of Sunset Boulevard and Baroda Drive.

G   And so a map was needed.

H   It is the oldest continuously published star map and one of a half-dozen or so maps of varying degrees of accuracy and spelling correctness sold today.

PART 3

You are going to read a magazine article about baseball. For questions 16–30, choose from the sections of the article (A–F). The sections may be chosen more than once. When more than one answer is required, these may be given in any order.

Mark your answers on the separate answer sheet.

In which section of the article are the following mentioned?

a game that may or may not have been baseball	16	17
the reason why a false story about the history of baseball was made public		18
a past belief that it was not worth keeping records on matters such as baseball		19
the importance of baseball in people's lives		20
the discovery of a document indicating that baseball existed even earlier than had previously been thought		21
uncertainty as to what future investigations of the origins of baseball will focus on		22
a belief that the true origin of baseball might never be firmly established		23
a generally accepted belief about the origin of baseball that was shown to be false	24	25
a belief that baseball developed gradually rather than having a single starting point		26
a contrast between what is known about baseball and what is known about well-known people in US history	27	28
the enormous importance of facts and records in baseball		29
the identification of an individual who was claimed to be the inventor of baseball		30

TEST 4

The origins of baseball

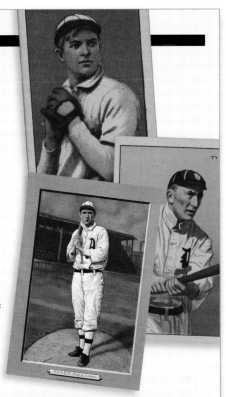

A Textbooks once stated with complete certainty that baseball was invented in Cooperstown, New York, in 1839, and provided as proof the picture of a dusty, ripped ball pulled from an attic trunk. It turned out to be a hoax. The next official version put the origin in Hoboken, New Jersey, in 1846. That story stood until 2001, when a librarian found two 1823 newspaper references to baseball games in Lower Manhattan. Then, in May 2004, a clerk walked out of a library vault in Pittsfield, Massachusetts, waving a faded ordinance from 1791 that banned the playing of baseball within 72 meters of the big church in the town square. Which raises the question: How come history can say what John Adams, America's second president, had for lunch on January 24, 1776 (wild goose), but baseball cannot pinpoint its origins to within hundreds of years or thousands of kilometers?

B For baseball, there is no agreement on which century the first game was played. It could have been the 18th century; it could have been the 13th century. There is some record of each. There is no agreement on which continent baseball was invented in. Was it North America, Europe or Africa? There is evidence for all three. 'With a sport like baseball, which so cares about statistics and its past,' the historian Doris Kearnes Goodwin said, 'you would think that this major detail of the past would be the crown jewel to find. Baseball, after all, is the ultimate sport of figures and dates. The origin of the game is the fabulous treasure.'

C 'People ask: when was the first baseball game?' said John Thorn, the baseball historian who uncovered the existence of the Pittsfield ordinance during a middle-of-the-night Internet search. 'It may be an unanswerable question. That's what makes it eternally fascinating.' Tom Shieber, the curator of new media at the National Baseball Hall of Fame in Cooperstown, New York, said: 'We know there were ball-games going back many centuries. There is a reference to the Pilgrims at Plymouth Rock playing ball. But was it baseball as we know it? And what is that?' Ted Spencer, the Hall of Fame's longtime curator, added another perspective. 'Did you know the Pittsfield ordinance also bans another bunch of sports, including football?' Mr Spencer said. 'Did you know nobody cares? But they care that it mentioned baseball. I got calls from reporters all over the country. That's because baseball has a spiritual hold on the American public.'

D The most commonly-accepted theory is that baseball has no specific starting date or place of invention. The game, they say, evolved over time. Still, it does raise some fundamental questions: Why has baseball's earliest history been so undiscovered? Why is it that the small details of the lives of celebrated American pioneers are so public but until recently little was done to trace baseball before 1823? 'Because the daily lives of prominent leaders in the American colonies were considered important and someone wrote the details down,' said Mr Shieber. 'But the games were child's play and often regarded as a wasteful use of time. They weren't documented in the same way.'

E Placing the origin of baseball in Cooperstown in 1839 was the work of a turn-of-the-century commission empowered by A.G. Spalding, the sports goods businessman, who influenced the findings to ensure the sport had, in his words at the time, 'an American dad'. That became Doubleday, an officer during the American Civil War, who was supposed to have laid out the first baseball field in Cooperstown. In the latter half of the 20th century, this tale was totally discredited. Baseball researchers now focus their energy on disproving other myths, like the long-held belief that baseball evolved from the English game of rounders.

F At the Hall of Fame, Mr. Spencer pointed to a reproduction hanging on a wall. It is a drawing from Spain in 1251 of people playing a game. 'There's a bat and there's a ball,' he said, looking at the drawing. 'It looks like two guys playing baseball to me.' Not far away is another reproduction of an Egyptian wall inscription: pharaohs perhaps engaged in another ball game. 'I guess the searching could go in any direction,' Ms. Goodwin said, 'though it's hard to imagine John Adams playing baseball. But you never know.' On page 31 of David McCullough's biography *John Adams*, Adams describes in his diary his idyllic boyhood activities: 'making and sailing boats' and 'swimming, skating, flying kites and shooting marbles, bat and ball.' John Adams was born in 1735.

Paper 2: Writing (1 hour 20 minutes)

PART 1

*You **must** answer this question. Write your answer in 120–150 words in an appropriate style.*

1 You have received an email from a friend from an English-speaking country, Max, who recently stayed with you. During his visit, he met your friends. Read Max's email and the notes you have made. Then write an email to Max, using **all** your notes.

---

email **page 1 of 1**

From:	Max Spicer
Sent:	2nd March
Subject:	How is everyone?

they felt the same ↗

I really enjoyed my time with you and it was great meeting all your friends. I'd love to hear some news about them.

How are Tim and Eddie? Have they still got their band? I thought they were really good. Have they played anywhere since I was there?

→ *yes and yes — tell him about concert*

And what about Ruth? Did she get that job in the museum? I know she really wanted it.

→ *yes and . . .*

What are Richard and Anna doing? Have they gone travelling? I think they said they were planning to do that.

yes, say where

I often think about you all and what a great time I had. Please keep me up to date on everyone.

Max

Write your **email**. You must use grammatically correct sentences with accurate spelling and punctuation in a style appropriate for the situation.

Write an answer to one of the questions 2–5 in this part. Write your answer in 120–180 words in an appropriate style.

2   You recently saw this notice in an English-language magazine.

> ### THE GAMES PEOPLE PLAY
>
> Write a review of a game that you played recently. It doesn't have to be a new game. You could review a computer game, or any other indoor game such as a board game. Describe the game and give us your opinions on it. Is it exciting? Is it hard to be good at it? If it's a popular game, why is it popular, in your opinion? We'll publish some of the reviews in a special section about games around the world.

Write your review.

3   You have seen this announcement in an English-language magazine.

> ### ARE YOU A WINNER?
>
> Have you ever entered a competition or a sports tournament? Write and tell us about your experiences. Tell us about the competition or tournament. Did you enjoy it? Did you expect to win? Did you win? If so, what was the prize? If not, how did you feel? We'll publish the best letters in a special Letters Page.

Write your letter.

4   Your teacher has asked you to write an essay on the following topic.

It is important that people choose a career when they are still quite young.

Write your essay.

5   Answer one of the following two questions based on your reading of one of the set books.

Either

5(a) Write an essay describing how a relationship between characters in the book changes. In what ways does it change and why does it change?

Or

(5b) Write the story of what happens to one of the characters in the book, concentrating on that particular character.

TEST 4

Paper 3: Use of English (45 minutes)

PART 1

For questions 1–12, read the text below and decide which answer (A, B, C or D) best fits each gap. There is an example at the beginning (0).

Mark your answers on the separate answer sheet.

Example:

0 A notice   **B** attention   **C** regard   **D** interest

0	A	**B**	C	D

She studies while he plays: true of children and chimps

Little girls watch and learn; little boys don't pay 0_____ and play around. At least, this seems to be the 1_____ with chimpanzees, according to new research.

Chimpanzees in the wild 2_____ to snack on termites, and youngsters learn to fish for them by poking long sticks and other 3_____ tools into the mounds that large groups of termites build. Researchers found that 4_____ average female chimps in the Gombe National Park in Tanzania learnt how to do termite fishing at the age of 31 months, more than two years earlier than the males.

The females seem to learn by watching their mothers. Researcher Dr. Elisabeth V. Lonsdorf, director of field conservation at the Lincoln Park Zoo in Chicago, said that it is 5_____ to find

that, when a young male and female are near a mound, 'she's really focusing on termite fishing and he's spinning himself round 6_____ circles.' Dr. Lansdorf and colleagues are studying chimpanzees at the zoo with a new, 7_____ created termite mound, filled with mustard 8_____ than termites. On the first day, adult females were getting at the mustard and a young female watched carefully and began to 9_____ the skills. Two young males did not do as well as the females – one simply sat next to his mother and tried to 10_____ some mustard from her, Dr. Lansdorf said. The behaviour of both sexes may seem 11_____ to many parents, she said, adding, 'The sex differences we found in the chimps are 12_____ to some of the findings from human child development research.'

1	**A** case	**B** matter	**C** fact	**D** event
2	**A** delight	**B** enjoy	**C** like	**D** fancy
3	**A** relative	**B** connected	**C** close	**D** similar
4	**A** on	**B** by	**C** at	**D** for
5	**A** ordinary	**B** regular	**C** typical	**D** frequent
6	**A** with	**B** in	**C** to	**D** through
7	**A** specially	**B** particularly	**C** singly	**D** distinctly
8	**A** other	**B** else	**C** rather	**D** instead
9	**A** pick up	**B** find out	**C** come to	**D** take on
10	**A** rob	**B** grasp	**C** grip	**D** steal
11	**A** acquainted	**B** familiar	**C** recognized	**D** known
12	**A** corresponding	**B** alike	**C** identical	**D** matching

*For questions 13–24, read the text below and think of the word which best fits each gap. Use only **one** word in each gap. There is an example at the beginning (0).*

Write your answers IN CAPITAL LETTERS on the separate answer sheet.

Example:

0	A	T												

NATIONAL VEGETARIAN WEEK

Around 5% of British households now have **0**_____ least one family member who is vegetarian, **13**_____ means that in the region of 3 million British people are vegetarians. About 25% of all females **14**_____ the ages of 16 and 24 are vegetarian.

Vegetarians do not eat meat, fish or poultry. Among the many reasons **15**_____ being a vegetarian are health, compassion for animals, and religious beliefs.

A vegetarian diet can meet **16**_____ known nutrient needs. The key to a healthy vegetarian diet, as with **17**_____ other diet, is to eat a wide variety of foods, including fruits, vegetables, plenty of leafy greens, whole-grain products, nuts, seeds and legumes. Sweets and fatty foods should **18**_____ limited.

Statistically, if you choose **19**_____ diet, you are choosing an option which should boost your chances of living a long and healthy life. But why? The reason **20**_____ that a good vegetarian diet contains more carbohydrate, more vitamin C and more fibre **21**_____ one where a high proportion of the calories come from meat.

There is documentary evidence of a Vegetarian Day **22**_____ held as early as 1936, but National Vegetarian Week **23**_____ we know it today has its roots in the National Vegetarian Day held by the Vegetarian Society in October 1991. It proved **24**_____ successful that they extended it to a whole week.

PART 3

For questions 25–34, read the text below. Use the word given in capitals at the end of some of the lines to form a word that fits in the gap in the same line. There is an example at the beginning (0).

Write your answers IN CAPITAL LETTERS *on the separate answer sheet.*

Example:

0	L	E	A	D	I	N	G							

WHEN BOSSES MAKE SPEECHES

For business managers, public speaking is part of the job. A survey of

100 **0** _____ companies found that chief executives received on   LEAD

average 175 **25** _____ a year to speak at conferences. Some   INVITE

executives love public speaking but some have an enormous

26 _____ for it.   LIKE

    There are plenty of experts giving **27** _____ to them on how to   ADVISE

interest **28** _____ . According to Carmine Gallo, author of a book   LISTEN

on public speaking, it is essential to avoid giving too much information

and to keep the audience's **29** _____ . He points to the example of   ATTEND

John Chambers, the chief executive of Cisco Systems, whose

30 _____ involves walking off the stage and into the audience, where   TECHNICAL

he asks a question or rests a hand on a person's shoulder in the style of a

television talk-show host. Speaking without notes, he **31** _____ that   SURE

he maintains constant eye contact with his audience.

    And then there is the **32** _____ public speaker Herbert D Kelleher,   LEGEND

former chief executive of Southwest Airlines. He would gather his ideas

33 _____ before a speech, jotting notes on a pad. 'People would ask   SHORT

after he spoke, "Can I have a copy of the speech?",' said Edward Stewart,

senior director of public relations at Southwest. 'We'd say, "**34** _____ ,   FORTUNATE

even Herb doesn't have a copy".'

PART 4

For questions 35–42, complete the second sentence so that it has a similar meaning to the first sentence, using the word given. Do not change the word given. You must use between two and five words, including the word given. Here is an example (0).

Example:

0 Making new friends was easy for her.

DIFFICULT

She didn't _____ new friends.

The gap can be filled with the words 'find it difficult to make', so you write:

| 0 | F | I | N | D | | I | T | | D | I | F | F | I | C | U | L | T | | T | O | | M | A | K | E | | |

Write the missing words IN CAPITAL LETTERS *on the separate answer sheet.*

---

35 It says here that we should we reply to this invitation.

SUPPOSED

It says here that _____ to this invitation.

36 I haven't got my wallet – it must be at home.

LEFT

I haven't got my wallet – I _____ at home.

37 The problem was that I hadn't expected it to take so long to get to the airport.

LONGER

The problem was that _____ I had expected to get to the airport.

38 Is it likely that this invention will become popular with the public?

CATCH

Is this invention likely _____ with the public?

39 I was driving home from work when the accident happened.

TIME

I was driving home from work _____ the accident.

40 There are a minimum of seven classes a week during the course.

LEAST

The course consists _____ seven classes a week.

41 My sister can't drive so she hasn't got her own car.

KNOW

My sister _____ drive so she hasn't got her own car.

42 I wrote down his email address on a piece of paper.

NOTE

I _____ his email address on a piece of paper.

Paper 4: Listening (40 minutes)

PART 1

You will hear people talking in eight different situations. For questions 1–8, choose the best answer, (A, B or C).

1   You hear someone talking on a radio programme.
    What is the speaker doing?

    A   recommending that listeners make a certain drink

    B   explaining why a drink is becoming more popular   [1]

    C   telling listeners about a drink they may not know about

2   You hear someone talking about people who travel a lot when they're young.
    What is his attitude towards these people?

    A   He is envious of them for having the opportunity.

    B   He feels that they are simply wasting their time.   [2]

    C   He can't understand why they do it.

3   You hear an advertisement for a course.
    What does the speaker say about the course?

    A   You need to take a test before being accepted for it.

    B   It starts with theory and moves on to practical work.   [3]

    C   It focuses on your effect on the people you will instruct.

4   You hear part of a radio interview.
    Who is being interviewed?

    A   a film director

    B   an actor   [4]

    C   a screenwriter

TEST 4

5 You hear part of a radio report about car drivers.
   What did the survey discover about a lot of drivers?

   A They pay no attention to warning lights.

   B They don't know what various symbols in a car relate to.   [5]

   C They think there are too many warning lights and symbols in cars.

6 You turn on the radio and hear part of a programme.
   What type of programme is it?

   A a review programme

   B a chat show   [6]

   C a phone-in

7 You hear part of a radio play.
   Where is the scene taking place?

   A in a restaurant

   B in a car   [7]

   C in a house

8 You hear a woman talking about running.
   What aspect of running is she talking about?

   A her involvement in running over a period of time

   B why she finds running so enjoyable   [8]

   C the importance of running and training with others

TEST 4

PART 2

You will hear an announcement about a competition. For questions 9–18, complete the sentences.

THE IDEAS COMPETITION

The money given to the winner is not a [_____ **9**].

The winner might be [_____ **10**] with a plan for improving a water supply.

The winner might have an idea about how to help the [_____ **11**] in the world.

If you enter the competition by phone you must explain your idea in a maximum of [_____ **12**].

One of the categories is for people who want to start a business that provides a [_____ or _____ **13**] that currently doesn't exist.

One of the categories is for people who want to take part in a project that is [_____ **14**].

One of the rules is that [_____ **15**] for the competition are not allowed.

Before you phone, it may be a good idea to prepare a [_____ **16**].

To win, you must show that you have a lot of [_____ **17**] for your idea.

Judges will listen to the ideas presented by [_____ **18**] people.

You will hear five different people talking about how they felt when they received an award.
For questions 19–23, choose from the list (A–F) how each person felt. Use the letters only
once. There is one extra letter which you do not need to use.

A   relieved

Speaker 1 | 19

B   worried

Speaker 2 | 20

C   proud

Speaker 3 | 21

D   exhausted

Speaker 4 | 22

E   grateful

Speaker 5 | 23

F   confused

TEST 4

PART 4

You will hear an interview with someone who has started a magazine for children. For questions 24–30, choose the best answer (A, B or C).

24 When talking about her job as a primary school teacher, Kate emphasizes
   A how much effort the job required.
   B how good she was as a teacher.
   C how difficult the children could be.

24

25 Kate decided to start her own magazine for children
   A because both children and parents suggested the idea.
   B when she was working in publishing for children.
   C after considering what was available for children.

25

26 What does Kate say about enthusiasm?
   A Children respond positively to it.
   B Children cannot maintain it for long.
   C Children experience it more than adults.

26

27 Kate says that she learnt from her research that children
   A don't want to feel that they are being considered inferior.
   B don't like texts that have too much serious content.
   C don't know some words that she had expected them to know.

27

28 Kate says that the age range for the magazine
   A may change to some extent in the future.
   B may not be exactly what it is stated to be.
   C has been decided after asking parents.

28

29 Kate says that the magazine makes use of the Internet because
   A some children prefer using it to learn about subjects.
   B some subjects cannot be covered fully in the magazine.
   C it is used a great deal in connection with some school work.

29

30 Kate says that one of her aims for the magazine is to
   A include subjects that children don't normally read about.
   B create an interest in subjects some children consider boring.
   C encourage children to choose what they want as a career.

30

Paper 5: Speaking (14 minutes)

<u>PART 1</u> (3 minutes)

Music

- What's your favourite kind of music? ..... (Why?)
- What kind(s) of music don't you like? ..... (Why?)
- What kinds of music are popular with young people in your country? ..... (Why?)
- Have you ever tried to play a musical instrument? Did you do well?
- Which instrument(s) would you like to be able to play? ..... (Why?)

Technology / Gadgets

- What pieces of technology or electronic gadgets do you own?
- How did you learn how to use pieces of technology or electronic gadgets?
- What do you think are the advantages and disadvantages of new technology for communicating with other people? ..... (Why?)
- Which pieces of technology or electronic gadgets would you like to own? ..... (Why?)

1 Working life
2 Visiting a city

Candidate A	Look at the two photographs 1A and 1B on page 127. They show people working.
	Compare the photographs and say what the people's working lives are like.
	Candidate A talks on his / her own for about 1 minute.
Candidate B	Which of the situations would you prefer to be in, and why?
	Candidate B talks on his / her own for about 20 seconds.
Candidate B	Look at the two photographs 2A and 2B on page 127. They show visitors to a city.
	Compare the photographs and say what kind of trips the people are on.
	Candidate B talks on his / her own for about 1 minute.
Candidate A	Which of the trips would you prefer to take?
	Candidate A talks on his / her own for about 20 seconds.

A day with a visitor

PART 3

Imagine that a friend of yours has a friend from another country staying with him / her. Your friend has to go out for a day next week and has asked you to look after the visitor for a day. Look at the ideas for what you could do with the visitor for that day on page 128.

First, talk to each other about whether each of the ideas would be good for the visitor and good for you. Then decide which two activities to do with the visitor and plan the day.

Candidates A and B discuss this together for about 3 minutes.

PART 4

- If a visitor from another country came to stay with you, what would be the first place you would take that person to? ..... (Why?)
- What place(s) would you certainly not take a visitor to? ..... (Why?)
- Do many overseas visitors come to your country? ..... (Why? / Why not?)
- When you go out with friends, what sort of places do you go to and what do you do there?
- How active are young people in your country? Do they prefer to do things that involve sitting down for long periods?
- What entertainment is available in the place where you live? What other kinds of entertainment do you think should be available?
- Some people say that too much entertainment is available to people and so they are unable to entertain themselves. Do you agree?

TEST 4

 UNIVERSITY *of* CAMBRIDGE
ESOL Examinations

Do not write in this box

Candidate Name
If not already printed, write name
in CAPITALS and complete the
Candidate No. grid (in pencil).

Candidate Signature

SAMPLE

Examination Title

Centre

Supervisor:
If the candidate is ABSENT or has WITHDRAWN shade here ▭

Centre No.

Candidate No.

Examination
Details

Candidate Answer Sheet

Instructions

Use a PENCIL (B or HB).

Mark ONE letter for each question.

For example, if you think B is the right answer to the question, mark your answer sheet like this:

0 A B C D E F G H

Rub out any answer you wish to change using an eraser.

1	A B C D E F G H
2	A B C D E F G H
3	A B C D E F G H
4	A B C D E F G H
5	A B C D E F G H
6	A B C D E F G H
7	A B C D E F G H
8	A B C D E F G H
9	A B C D E F G H
10	A B C D E F G H
11	A B C D E F G H
12	A B C D E F G H
13	A B C D E F G H
14	A B C D E F G H
15	A B C D E F G H
16	A B C D E F G H
17	A B C D E F G H
18	A B C D E F G H
19	A B C D E F G H
20	A B C D E F G H

21	A B C D E F G H
22	A B C D E F G H
23	A B C D E F G H
24	A B C D E F G H
25	A B C D E F G H
26	A B C D E F G H
27	A B C D E F G H
28	A B C D E F G H
29	A B C D E F G H
30	A B C D E F G H
31	A B C D E F G H
32	A B C D E F G H
33	A B C D E F G H
34	A B C D E F G H
35	A B C D E F G H
36	A B C D E F G H
37	A B C D E F G H
38	A B C D E F G H
39	A B C D E F G H
40	A B C D E F G H

A-H 40 CAS

denote
Print Limited 0121 520 5100

DP594/300

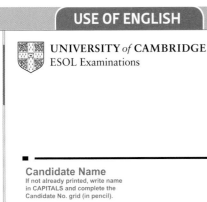

UNIVERSITY *of* **CAMBRIDGE**
ESOL Examinations

Do not write in this box

Candidate Name
If not already printed, write name
in CAPITALS and complete the
Candidate No. grid (in pencil).

Candidate Signature

Examination Title

Centre

Supervisor:

If the candidate is ABSENT or has WITHDRAWN shade here ▭

SAMPLE

Centre No.

Candidate No.

Examination
Details

Candidate Answer Sheet

Instructions

Use a PENCIL (B or HB). Rub out any answer you wish to change using an eraser.

Part 1: Mark ONE letter for each question.

For example, if you think **B** is the right
answer to the question, mark your
answer sheet like this:

Parts 2, 3 and **4:** Write your answer clearly
in CAPITAL LETTERS.

For Parts 2 and 3 write one letter
in each box. For example:

Part 1				
1	A	B	C	D
2	A	B	C	D
3	A	B	C	D
4	A	B	C	D
5	A	B	C	D
6	A	B	C	D
7	A	B	C	D
8	A	B	C	D
9	A	B	C	D
10	A	B	C	D
11	A	B	C	D
12	A	B	C	D

Part 2

Do not write
below here

13
14
15
16
17
18
19
20
21
22
23
24

Continues over ➡

FCE UoE

DP596/305

Part 3

Do not write below here

25		25 1 0 u
26		26 1 0 u
27		27 1 0 u
28		28 1 0 u
29		29 1 0 u
30		30 1 0 u
31		31 1 0 u
32		32 1 0 u
33		33 1 0 u
34		34 1 0 u

Part 4

Do not write below here

SAMPLE

35		35 2 1 0 u
36		36 2 1 0 u
37		37 2 1 0 u
38		38 2 1 0 u
39		39 2 1 0 u
40		40 2 1 0 u
41		41 2 1 0 u
42		42 2 1 0 u

denote
Print Limited 0121 520 5100

UNIVERSITY *of* **CAMBRIDGE**
ESOL Examinations

> Do not write in this box

Candidate Name
If not already printed, write name
in CAPITALS and complete the
Candidate No. grid (in pencil).

Candidate Signature

Examination Title

Centre

SAMPLE

Centre No.

Candidate No.

**Examination
Details**

0	0	0	0
1	1	1	1
2	2	2	2
3	3	3	3
4	4	4	4
5	5	5	5
6	6	6	6
7	7	7	7
8	8	8	8
9	9	9	9

Supervisor:

If the candidate is ABSENT or has WITHDRAWN shade here ▭

Test version: A B C D E F J K L M N   Special arrangements: S H

Candidate Answer Sheet

Instructions

Use a PENCIL (B or HB).
Rub out any answer you wish to change using an eraser.

Parts 1, 3 and 4:
Mark ONE letter for each question.

For example, if you think **B** is the
right answer to the question, mark
your answer sheet like this:

    0   A B C

Part 2:
Write your answer clearly in CAPITAL LETTERS.

Write one letter or number in each box.
If the answer has more than one word, leave one
box empty between words.

For example:

    0 N U M B E R   1 2

Turn this sheet over to start.

FCE L

Part 1

	A	B	C
1			
2			
3			
4			
5			
6			
7			
8			

Part 2 (Remember to write in CAPITAL LETTERS or numbers)

Do not write below here

		1 0 u
9	SAMPLE	9
10		10
11		11
12		12
13		13
14		14
15		15
16		16
17		17
18		18

Part 3

	A	B	C	D	E	F
19						
20						
21						
22						
23						

Part 4

	A	B	C
24			
25			
26			
27			
28			
29			
30			

denote Print Limited 0121 520 5100

TEST 1

Paper 1: Reading

PART 1		16
PART 2		14
PART 3		15

Total [ ] **45**   Score [ ] 40

Candidate score x 9 ÷ 10 = score out of 40
Example: 36 marks out of 45 = 32 marks out of 40 approximately.

Paper 2: Writing

PART 1		20
PART 2		20

Total [ ] **40**   Score [ ] 40

Paper 3: Use of English

PART 1		12
PART 2		12
PART 3		10
PART 4		16

Total [ ] **50**   Score [ ] 40

Candidate score x 8 ÷ 10 = score out of 40
Example: 38 marks out of 50 = 30 marks out of 40 approximately

Paper 4: Listening

PART 1		8
PART 2		10
PART 3		5
PART 4		7

Total [ ] **30**   Score [ ] 40

Candidate score ÷ 3 x 4 = score out of 40
Example: 24 marks out of 30 = 32 marks out of 40

Paper 5: Speaking

Total [ ] **20**   Score [ ] 40

Candidate score x 2 = score out of 40

Test total [ ] 200
÷ 2 = [ ] %
Approximate grade (see below) [ ]

TEST 2

Paper 1: Reading

PART 1		16
PART 2		14
PART 3		15

Total [ ] **45**   Score [ ] 40

Candidate score x 9 ÷ 10 = score out of 40
Example: 36 marks out of 45 = 32 marks out of 40 approximately.

Paper 2: Writing

PART 1		20
PART 2		20

Total [ ] **40**   Score [ ] 40

Paper 3: Use of English

PART 1		12
PART 2		12
PART 3		10
PART 4		16

Total [ ] **50**   Score [ ] 40

Candidate score x 8 ÷ 10 = score out of 40
Example: 38 marks out of 50 = 30 marks out of 40 approximately

Paper 4: Listening

PART 1		8
PART 2		10
PART 3		5
PART 4		7

Total [ ] **30**   Score [ ] 40

Candidate score ÷ 3 x 4 = score out of 40
Example: 24 marks out of 30 = 32 marks out of 40

Paper 5: Speaking

Total [ ] **20**   Score [ ] 40

Candidate score x 2 = score out of 40

Test total [ ] 200
÷ 2 = [ ] %
Approximate grade (see below) [ ]

Approximate percentages for grades A–E

Pass	A	80% and above	**Fail**	D	55–59%
	B	75–79%		E	54% and below
	C	60–74%			

TEST 3

Paper 1: Reading

PART 1 [ ] 16
PART 2 [ ] 14
PART 3 [ ] 15

Total [ ] **45**   Score [ ] 40

Candidate score x 9 ÷ 10 = score out of 40
Example: 36 marks out of 45 = 32 marks out of 40 approximately.

Paper 2: Writing

PART 1 [ ] 20
PART 2 [ ] 20

Total [ ] **40**   Score [ ] 40

Paper 3: Use of English

PART 1 [ ] 12
PART 2 [ ] 12
PART 3 [ ] 10
PART 4 [ ] 16

Total [ ] **50**   Score [ ] 40

Candidate score x 8 ÷ 10 = score out of 40
Example: 38 marks out of 50 = 30 marks out of 40 approximately

Paper 4: Listening

PART 1 [ ] 8
PART 2 [ ] 10
PART 3 [ ] 5
PART 4 [ ] 7

Total [ ] **30**   Score [ ] 40

Candidate score ÷ 3 x 4 = score out of 40
Example: 24 marks out of 30 = 32 marks out of 40

Paper 5: Speaking

Total [ ] **20**   Score [ ] 40

Candidate score x 2 = score out of 40

Test total [ ]	200
÷ 2 = [ ]	%
Approximate grade (see below) [ ]	

TEST 4

Paper 1: Reading

PART 1 [ ] 16
PART 2 [ ] 14
PART 3 [ ] 15

Total [ ] **45**   Score [ ] 40

Candidate score x 9 ÷ 10 = score out of 40
Example: 36 marks out of 45 = 32 marks out of 40 approximately.

Paper 2: Writing

PART 1 [ ] 20
PART 2 [ ] 20

Total [ ] **40**   Score [ ] 40

Paper 3: Use of English

PART 1 [ ] 12
PART 2 [ ] 12
PART 3 [ ] 10
PART 4 [ ] 16

Total [ ] **50**   Score [ ] 40

Candidate score x 8 ÷ 10 = score out of 40
Example: 38 marks out of 50 = 30 marks out of 40 approximately

Paper 4: Listening

PART 1 [ ] 8
PART 2 [ ] 10
PART 3 [ ] 5
PART 4 [ ] 7

Total [ ] **30**   Score [ ] 40

Candidate score ÷ 3 x 4 = score out of 40
Example: 24 marks out of 30 = 32 marks out of 40

Paper 5: Speaking

Total [ ] **20**   Score [ ] 40

Candidate score x 2 = score out of 40

Test total [ ]	200
÷ 2 = [ ]	%
Approximate grade (see below) [ ]	

Approximate percentages for grades A–E

Pass   **A**   80% and above   **Fail**   **D**   55–59%
      B   75–79%   **E**   54% and below
      C   60–74%

Assessing the Writing paper

Students' answers are assessed with reference to two mark schemes: one based on the overall impression; the other on the requirements of the particular task.

The General impression mark scheme refers to the content, organization and cohesion, range of structures and vocabulary, accuracy, register and format, and the target reader indicated in the task.

The Task specific mark scheme in the Answer key lists the criteria specific to each particular task and explains what is required in each answer. Teachers should assess the answer under the Task specific mark scheme and then award an overall General impression band mark and a score out of 20.

Candidates who fully satisfy the Band 3 descriptor will demonstrate an adequate performance in writing at FCE level.

General impression mark scheme

BAND 5 *(approximately 17–20 marks)*

For a Band 5 to be awarded, the candidate's writing fully achieves the desired effect on the target reader. All the content points required in the task are included and expanded appropriately. Ideas are organized effectively, with the use of a variety of linking devices and a wide range of structure and vocabulary. The language is well developed, and any errors that do occur are minimal and perhaps due to ambitious attempts at more complex language. Register and format which is consistently appropriate to the purpose of the task and the audience is used.

BAND 4 *(approximately 13–16 marks)*

For a Band 4 to be awarded, the candidate's writing achieves the desired effect on the target reader. All the content points required in the task are included. Ideas are clearly organized, with the use of suitable linking devices and a good range of structure and vocabulary. Generally, the language is accurate, and any errors that do occur are mainly due to attempts at more complex language. Register and format which is, on the whole, appropriate to the purpose of the task and the audience is used.

BAND 3 *(approximately 8–12 marks)*

For a Band 3 to be awarded, the candidate's writing, on the whole, achieves the desired effect on the target reader. All the content points required in the task are included. Ideas are organized adequately, with the use of simple linking devices and an adequate range of structure and vocabulary. A number of errors may be present, but they do not impede communication. A reasonable, if not always successful, attempt is made at register and format which is appropriate to the purpose of the task and the audience.

BAND 2 *(approximately 4–7 marks)*

For a Band 2 to be awarded, the candidate's writing does not clearly communicate the message to the target reader. Some content points required in the task are inadequately covered or omitted, and/or there is some irrelevant material. Ideas are inadequately organized, linking devices are rarely used, and the range of structure and vocabulary is limited. Errors distract the reader and may obscure communication at times. Attempts at appropriate register and format are unsuccessful or inconsistent.

BAND 1 *(approximately 1–3 marks)*

For a Band 1 to be awarded, the candidate's writing has a very negative effect on the target reader. There is notable omission of content points and/or considerable irrelevance, possibly due to misinterpretation of the task. There is a lack of organization or linking devices, and there is little evidence of language control. The range of structure and vocabulary is narrow, and frequent errors obscure communication. There is little or no awareness of appropriate register and format.

BAND 0 *(no marks)*

For a Band zero to be awarded, there is either too little language for assessment or the candidate's writing is totally irrelevant or totally illegible.

Assessing the Speaking paper

Assessment (out of 20 marks) is based on performance in the whole test, and is not related to performance in particular parts of the test. Students are assessed on their own performance, and not in relation to each other.

Marks are awarded by the assessor, who does not take part in the test, according to four analytical criteria: *Grammar and Vocabulary*, *Discourse Management*, *Pronunciation*, and *Interactive Communication*. The interlocutor, who conducts the test, gives a mark for *Global Achievement*.

GRAMMAR AND VOCABULARY

This refers to the accurate and appropriate use of a range of grammatical forms and vocabulary. Performance is viewed in terms of the overall effectiveness of the language used in spoken interaction.

DISCOURSE MANAGEMENT

This refers to the candidate's ability to link utterances together to form coherent speech, without undue hesitation. The utterances should be relevant to the tasks and should be arranged logically to develop the themes or arguments required by the tasks.

PRONUNCIATION

This refers to the candidate's ability to produce intelligible utterances to fulfil the task requirements. This includes stress and intonation as well as individual sounds. Examiners put themselves in the position of a non-ESOL specialist and assess the overall impact of the pronunciation and the degree of effort required to understand the candidate.

INTERACTIVE COMMUNICATION

This refers to the candidate's ability to take an active part in the development of the discourse. This requires an ability to participate in the range of interactive situations in the test and to develop discussions on a range of topics by initiating and responding appropriately. This also refers to the deployment of strategies to maintain interaction at an appropriate level throughout the test so that the tasks can be fulfilled.

GLOBAL ACHIEVEMENT

This refers to the candidate's overall effectiveness in dealing with the tasks in the four separate parts of the FCE Speaking test. The global mark is an independent impression mark which reflects the assessment of the candidate's performance from the interlocutor's perspective.

For an explanation of how marks are calculated, see the DIY Marksheets on page 91.

TEST 1

Paper 1: Reading

PART 1

1	B	5	B
2	A	6	C
3	C	7	C
4	D	8	B

PART 2

9	E	13	D
10	G	14	F
11	B	15	C
12	H		

PART 3

16	C	21	A	26	C
17	A	22	D	27	B
18	B	23	B	28	D
19	D	24	C	29	C
20	C	25	A	30	D

Paper 2: Writing

For General impression mark scheme see page 93.

QUESTION 1 *Task specific mark scheme*

Content

The letter must include everything in the notes, and therefore must include thanking the people for their offer, a brief description of the writer and the background to the letter, a suggested time for the visit and a request for information about things to see and do.

Range of grammar and vocabulary

The letter should include the correct use of these tenses: present continuous for the person's current situation, and future tenses (e.g. present continuous and *going to*) for future plans. It should also include the correct use of *would* in requests and in structures such as *would like* + infinitive and *would be grateful if*. Vocabulary connected with travel and plans should be used.

Register

The register should be fairly formal but friendly, as is appropriate for the situation of writing to someone you have never met about a social arrangement.

Organization and cohesion

An appropriate greeting at the beginning and end should be used. The greeting at the end may be less formal than *Yours sincerely*, because of the situation. The letter may be organized into short paragraphs dealing with different matters (the introduction giving thanks, the background to the visit and a suggested time for it, and the request for information).

Target reader

The reader would be pleased to get the letter, form a good impression of the person who has written it, and be clear as to what is required in their response to the letter.

Model answer

Dear Mr and Mrs Hampson,

Thank you for telling Olivia that I can visit you while I'm in Britain. It's very kind of you to offer and I would like to come and see you.

I'm 21 years old and I'm currently studying at university in my home town. I'm coming to Britain next month during my holiday from university. I'm going to stay with Olivia for some of the time and I'm also planning to go to other parts of Britain. It would be very nice to come to your part of Britain. Would it be convenient for me to come for a weekend at the end of August?

Please write back to me and tell me if my suggestion for when to visit you is fine with you. And I'd be grateful if you could also recommend some places for me to visit and interesting things that I can do while I'm in the Midlands.

Best wishes,

QUESTION 2 *Task specific mark scheme*

Content

The essay should fully address the points made in the statement, discussing both whether or not computer games are bad for people and the question of problems that they cause.

Range of grammar and vocabulary

It is likely that modal verbs such as *can, might, may*, etc. are required to talk about possible situations and the results of them. The present simple tense is likely to be required to talk about habits and general facts. Vocabulary connected with habits, leisure time and causes and results is required.

Register

The essay could be fairly formal, informal or neutral, depending on how the candidate wishes to approach the topic.

Organization and cohesion

The essay should be appropriately divided into paragraphs, separating points that agree with the statement in the question and points that disagree. Appropriate linking between different points should be used (e.g. *On the other hand*).

Target reader

The reader should understand fully the writer's opinions on the topic and the reasons why the writer has those opinions.

Model answer

It is true that computer games can be bad for some people. Many of the games are very violent and some people may be influenced by this and then do violent things themselves.

I also believe that computer games can be addictive and this can be bad for people. Some young people, for example, spend far too much time playing these games instead of activities that are much healthier for them, such as playing sports. This means that they can become unfit and also that they spend less time talking to their friends and having good relationships with other people.

Playing computer games for long periods of time can also have a bad effect on people psychologically. They can put people into a bad mood and affect their relationships with their friends and family.

On the other hand, computer games are not all bad. People can learn skills from playing them and of course they can be great fun. They provide a very good source of entertainment. There is nothing wrong with them as long as people don't spend too much time playing them.

QUESTION 3 *Task specific mark scheme*

Content

The article should explain what kind of performance it was, describe the performance, say whether it was successful or not, and describe the writer's feelings.

Range of grammar and vocabulary

The article should use appropriate past tenses, particularly the past simple and past perfect. Linkers connected with time (e.g. *when*, *before*, *after*) and causes and results (e.g. *because*) should be used correctly. Vocabulary connected with performing (e.g. music, acting, etc.) must be used appropriately. Vocabulary describing feelings must be used correctly.

Register

The article can be fairly informal or neutral – the announcement indicates this. It is for other people's entertainment.

Organization and cohesion

The article should be organized into paragraphs dealing with the kind of performance and the background to it, how the writer felt before it, what happened during it and how the writer felt then. It could also have a suitable title. Appropriate linking words and phrases for giving reasons and for describing a sequence of events should also be used.

Target reader

The reader should understand what the performance was and where it took place, what happened during it and how the writer felt at various times.

Model answer

MY BAND'S FIRST PERFORMANCE

I'm in a rock band with some of my friends and last year we did our first public performance. It was at a local festival. The guitarist's mother was one of the festival's organizers and that's why we had the chance to play there.

We were very nervous before we started playing because we had never played in public before. We'd done a lot of practising together and we knew all the songs very well but playing in front of an audience was totally different. We were worried that we might make a lot of mistakes and that people would think we were rubbish.

We played on a big stage and there were hundreds of people in the audience. When we finished the first song, they all clapped and cheered and this made us feel a lot better. I think we played very well and the audience seemed to enjoy our performance a lot. Afterwards, lots of people told us how good we were and that we would be famous one day! We were all extremely pleased and quite proud of ourselves.

QUESTION 4 *Task specific mark scheme*

Content

The review should describe the programme briefly and explain what the writer dislikes about it.

Range of grammar and vocabulary

The review should include appropriate structures for giving opinions and for expressing dislike. It should also include appropriate vocabulary for describing TV programmes (e.g. the people in them, what happens in them, etc.).

Register

The review can be informal or neutral. The notice indicates that the review should contain a totally personal reaction to a programme and that it might be amusing.

Organization and cohesion

The review may be divided into paragraphs, beginning with a description of the programme itself and then giving the writer's opinions of it. It may have a title (probably the name of the programme). Linking words and phrases should be used appropriately, particularly to link the writer's opinions with the reasons for them.

Target reader

The reader should have a clear idea of what the programme is like and why the writer dislikes it so much.

Model answer

INSIDE THE HOUSE

In my opinion this programme is the worst thing on TV at the moment and I simply cannot understand why anyone would want to watch it. In the programme, a group of young people who have never met each other before are sent to live in a big house in the middle of the countryside. The programme shows you how they get on with each other.

The main problem with this programme is that all the people in it are awful. They are all obviously desperate to be famous by appearing on TV but they are not interesting people at all. They talk about themselves all the time but they have very annoying personalities and their opinions are stupid. They are completely selfish and although they seem to think people watching them will find them fascinating, in fact I'm sure everyone at home is saying how terrible they are.

Another thing that makes the programme so annoying is that the people argue with each other all the time. It makes me just want to tell them all to shut up!

Paper 3: Use of English

PART 1

1	A	5	D	9	B
2	C	6	A	10	C
3	D	7	C	11	B
4	B	8	D	12	C

PART 2

13	since	17	when	21	the
14	after	18	too	22	makes
15	such	19	an	23	them
16	own	20	could	24	into

PART 3

25	outstanding	30	required
26	publicity	31	lowered
27	service	32	stability
28	considerably	33	colourful
29	wonderful	34	interests

PART 4

35 **even** though][he won
36 for][**quite** a long
37 to **get**][through
38 as **good** as][the first
39 would/do you **mind**][waiting
40 no **chance**][of getting
41 has a bad][**effect** on
42 nothing][**apart** from

Paper 4: Listening

PART 1

1	B	5	A
2	A	6	C
3	C	7	A
4	A	8	C

PART 2

9	social	14	ten/10 minutes
10	width	15	long; heavy
11	handler	16	lie down
12	pick up	17	attitude
13	nine/9	18	their ears

PART 3

19	A	22	C
20	E	23	D
21	F		

PART 4

24	B	28	A
25	A	29	C
26	B	30	A
27	C		

Paper 5: Speaking

Teachers should use their own judgement to award marks out of 20 based on the assessment criteria on page 94.

TEST 2

Paper 1: Reading

PART 1

1	B	5	B
2	C	6	D
3	C	7	B
4	A	8	D

PART 2

9	F	13	E
10	D	14	G
11	H	15	C
12	A		

PART 3

16	C	21	A	26	C
17	B	22	A	27	D
18	D	23	B	28	B
19	B	24	C	29	C
20	D	25	C	30	B

Paper 2: Writing

For General impression mark scheme see page 93.

QUESTION 1 *Task specific mark scheme*

Content

The email must include something relating to all of the notes – you should express sympathy at the beginning, suggest action about the work problem, suggest action about the problem with Helen and end with a message that George should feel better.

Range of grammar and vocabulary

The email should include the correct use of structures for giving advice (e.g. *should/ought to, why don't you, If I were you,* etc.) and for expressing feelings and opinions. Appropriate structures for describing impressions (e.g. *It seems to me*) can also be used.

Register

The email should be fairly informal because it is from one friend to another.

Organization and cohesion

The email should begin and end with references to the writer's and George's feelings. Each of the problems should be discussed separately, with advice on each one. A suitable phrase referring to a reply from George can be used. Appropriate linking words and phrases should be used (e.g. *As for*).

Target reader

The reader should understand that the writer sympathizes and wants the writer to feel better. The reader should be clear as to what the writer is suggesting to solve both problems.

Model answer

Hi George,

I'm sorry to hear that you're having such a bad time at the moment.

It seems to me that you need to take some action about your problems at work. I think you should talk to your boss immediately and explain the problem. It doesn't seem fair that you've got so much to do. Why don't you ask your boss to get someone else to help you or to do some of that work?

As for the problem with Helen, I'm sure you can sort that out, and that you don't need to split up. Of course, I don't know exactly what you said to her, but why don't you apologize to her? If I were you, I'd do that straight away. It's possible that she'll change her mind if you do that.

So, cheer up! I'm sure things will get better.

Let me know what happens.

QUESTION 2 *Task specific mark scheme*

Content

The report should describe events and changes in the place. It may refer to people in general or to specific people. It should include facts and it may also include comments on the events.

Range of grammar and vocabulary

The appropriate verb tenses should be used for describing past events and perhaps present situations resulting from them. Passive verb forms are likely to be required, because what happened may be more important than who did it. Comparative structures may be required. Appropriate vocabulary associated with the type of event described is required.

Register

The report should be fairly formal or neutral, because it deals mostly with facts and because the topic is a fairly serious one.

Organization and cohesion

The report may be divided into appropriate sections, each dealing with a different aspect. To make the report absolutely clear at a glance, these sections may be given titles, and the whole report may be given a title. Appropriate and varied use of linking words and phrases may be required (e.g. *This ... , However,* etc.)

Target reader

The reader should understand what kind of place is being described and what some of the most important events and changes were in that place in the last year. The reader may also understand the writer's opinions of these events.

Model answer

A YEAR IN THE LIFE OF PARKSIDE

Shopping

The most important event in the last year was probably the opening of the new shopping centre. It took some years for it to be built, but it finally opened in July. Most local people are very happy with it because we now have bigger shops than we used to have. However, other people say that it is not a good thing because some of the smaller shops in the town will have to close because of the new shopping centre.

Sport

Our football team did very well last season and got to the final of the National Cup competition. Thousands of us travelled to the National Stadium for the match and it was a fantastic day for the town. The team lost, but getting to the final for the first time was a great achievement for them.

Traffic

A new traffic system was introduced last year because the number of cars in the town centre had become too great and there was a lot of congestion. This has worked well and there are now fewer traffic jams in the centre.

QUESTION 3 *Task specific mark scheme*

Content

The story must have a beginning, a middle and an end, with the sentence given as the last sentence. It should make sense as a series of events and it should be clear exactly what happened. It should probably describe a fairly simple series of events. The final sentence should make sense with what has gone before in the story.

Range of grammar and vocabulary

The story must use the appropriate past tenses, particularly the past simple and perhaps the past continuous and the past perfect. Vocabulary appropriate to the subject of the story must be used accurately.

Register

The register should be neutral or fairly informal.

Organization and cohesion

The story should be organized so that the sequence of events is completely clear. This may involve suitable paragraphing. Appropriate linking words and phrases should be used to link the various events.

Target reader

The reader should be clear as to exactly what happens in the story and what the sequence of events is.

Model answer

Tom got into his car and drove away. It was an old car and Tom had bought it from a college friend. Tom's father had told him that he should have the car checked by a mechanic, but Tom hadn't done that.

Tom drove out into the countryside. It was a beautiful summer day, hot and sunny. There were no other cars on the road and Tom was enjoying the drive. The scenery was wonderful and everything was peaceful.

Suddenly, the car made a terrible noise and the engine stopped. Tom tried to start the engine again, but nothing happened. Now he was really in trouble. He was a long way from home, in a car that didn't work, and there was nobody around. He tried to phone his father on his mobile phone but it wasn't working either.

Tom walked for a very long time until, two hours later, he came to a village. There, he was able to use a phone to call his father, who came to collect him and arranged for the car to be taken away. It wasn't worth repairing it. After that, Tom promised himself that he would never make the same mistake again.

QUESTION 4 *Task specific mark scheme*

Content

The letter must name the person the writer would like to interview, say why the writer wants to interview that person and give examples of questions the writer would ask that person.

Range of grammar and vocabulary

The letter should use appropriate past and present tenses to talk about the person the writer would like to interview. Conditional structures are also likely to be required, and the modal *would* is likely to be required to talk about the hypothetical situation of interviewing the person. Vocabulary appropriate to the kind of person chosen (e.g. their work) is required and vocabulary connected with describing someone's personality may be required.

Register

The register may be neutral or fairly informal. The letter is to a magazine, not to an individual that the writer knows, and therefore it should not be too informal. However, the subject matter and situation mean that it should not be too formal.

Organization and cohesion

The letter may be divided into paragraphs dealing separately with the person chosen and the reason for that choice, and the questions to ask that person. Appropriate linking words and phrases should be used to link the writer's choices of person and questions with the reasons for those choices. The questions may be presented as a list, linked with words such as *also* and *Finally*.

Target reader

The reader would understand clearly why the writer has chosen the person and what the writer would ask the person in an interview.

Model answer

To the Editor,

The person I would really like to interview is the actress Gloria Johnson.

I would really like to interview her because I think she is the greatest actress in films today. I have seen all the films that she has starred in and I think that she is better than anyone else. Also, she has played a wide variety of roles in her films, and she has shown that she is a great actress in all of them. You believe that she really is that person in all her films.

If I could interview her, I would ask her about how she chooses which films she is going to appear in and how she prepares for each role. I would ask her what her favourite role has been. I would also like to know which actors she has enjoyed acting with and which ones she has not enjoyed acting with. Finally, I would ask her a few questions about her private life. She never talks about that in the interviews I've read but I hope that she would talk to me about it!

Yours sincerely

Paper 3: Use of English

PART 1

1	D	5	B	9	C
2	B	6	A	10	B
3	D	7	B	11	A
4	B	8	C	12	D

PART 2

13	back/backward(s)	19	for
14	As/When	20	and
15	each	21	most
16	so	22	whether/if
17	not	23	why
18	together	24	make/be

PART 3

25	stressful	30	memorable
26	commitments	31	helpful
27	solution	32	insights
28	accompanies	33	distinctive
29	personal	34	truly

PART 4

35 **instead** of][buying her a
36 is being][**run** by
37 don't/do not **give**][up
38 does it][**take** (you) to
39 were][no tickets **left** OR weren't][any tickets **left**
40 to **find** out][what
41 there is][a **sudden**
42 has never been][**happier** than

Paper 4: Listening

PART 1

1	B	4	A	7	C
2	A	5	A	8	B
3	B	6	B		

PART 2

9	underground systems	14	ear plugs
10	hairdryer	15	two-minute/2-minute
11	glass	16	ball of air
12	elbows; knees	17	smile machine
13	over/more than four/4	18	body flying

PART 3

19	D	21	A	23	E
20	F	22	C		

PART 4

24	C	28	A
25	A	29	B
26	B	30	C
27	B		

Paper 5: Speaking

Teachers should use their own judgement to award marks out of 20 based on the assessment criteria on page 94.

TEST 3

Paper 1: Reading

PART 1

1	B	5	B
2	D	6	D
3	A	7	A
4	C	8	C

PART 2

9	G	13	E
10	D	14	A
11	B	15	F
12	H		

PART 3

16	B	21	F	26	F
17	D	22	C	27	E
18	A	23	D	28	A
19	E	24	E	29	B
20	A	25	B	30	C

Paper 2: Writing

For General impression mark scheme see page 93.

QUESTION 1 *Task specific mark scheme*

Content

The letter should refer to the points made by the Branch Manager in her letter and include all the points made in the notes about these – the assistant's attitude, the time needed for the repair, the problems with the writer's computer and the writer's intention not to use the shop again.

Range of grammar and vocabulary

The letter should include appropriate verb tenses for describing what happened in the shop (especially the past simple), the general situation concerning the computer (present perfect or present simple), and the writer's future intention concerning using the shop. Vocabulary appropriate to shopping and the goods concerned should be used correctly, and vocabulary for expressing feeling and attitude should be used appropriately.

Register

The letter should be formal – it is a letter making a formal complaint to someone the writer does not know, in a formal context (business/shopping).

Organization and cohesion

The letter should begin with a short introduction referring to the letter from the manager and saying why the writer is writing to her again. It should deal with each point separately, and may be organized into appropriate paragraphs. Points should be linked appropriately (e.g. *Firstly, Secondly*). The difference between what the manager says in her letter and what the writer believes should be linked with appropriate words and phrases (e.g. *but, However*).

Target reader

The reader should understand clearly why the writer is not satisfied with the letter from the manager. The reader should understand fully the writer's version of events in the shop and how the writer feels about what has happened.

Model answer

Dear Ms Baker,

Thank you for your letter about my complaint. Unfortunately, I am not satisfied with your response.

You say that your assistant did his best to help me, but this is not true. In fact, he was quite rude to me and not at all helpful. Secondly, you say that your service guarantee makes it clear that repairs may take several days. In fact, it talks about 'speedy repairs' and so I was very surprised to find that my computer could not be repaired while I waited. I tried to explain that I knew what the problem was and that it could be fixed very quickly, but your assistant would not listen.

Concerning the quality of your products, all I can say is that I have had a lot of problems with the computer I bought from you. In view of that, and the way that I was treated by your assistant, I will certainly not be using your shop again.

Yours sincerely

QUESTION 2 *Task specific mark scheme*

Content

The story must contain a clear sequence of events and have a logical connection with the opening sentence.

Range of grammar and vocabulary

The story must use the appropriate past tenses, particularly the past simple and perhaps the past continuous and the past perfect. If appropriate, correct reported speech structures should be used. Vocabulary appropriate to the subject of the story must be used accurately.

Register

The register should be neutral or fairly informal.

Organization and cohesion

The story should be organized so that the sequence of events is completely clear – this may or may not require separate paragraphs. Appropriate linking words and phrases connected with time are required (e.g. *when, after, then*).

Target reader

The reader should be clear as to exactly what happens in the story and what the sequence of events is.

Model answer

When I started on the journey, I had no idea what was going to happen. I found my seat on the plane, sat down and then the plane took off. A man wearing dark glasses was sitting in the seat next to mine and after a few minutes he began talking to me. He asked me where I was going and why and we had a pleasant chat for a while. He told me that he was going to a special party. I asked him about the party and he said that it was for the opening of his latest film. We talked about the film and he said that he was the star of it. He told me that he was a very famous actor. Unfortunately, I didn't recognize him and I didn't know his name. He thought this was very funny and invited me to the party as his special guest. A few days later, I went to the party and some very famous people who I did recognize were there. It was quite an experience!

QUESTION 3 *Task specific mark scheme*

Content

The article must include all the aspects listed – what the hobby involves, why the writer likes it, why the writer started it, and how long the writer spends doing it.

Range of grammar and vocabulary

The article must use appropriate verb tenses – probably the present simple for what the hobby involves and perhaps the present perfect for the situation until now, as well as the past simple for the history of the hobby. Vocabulary connected with the hobby must be used accurately.

Register

The article can be fairly informal or neutral – the announcement indicates this. It is for other people's entertainment.

Organization and cohesion

The article should be organized so that each of the aspects listed is dealt with in a logical order – this does not have to be the same order as in the question.

Different aspects may be separated into different paragraphs. Appropriate linking words and phrases should be used to connect different aspects, to describe sequences of events and to give reasons.

Target reader

The reader should understand exactly what the hobby involves and why the writer enjoys it.

Model answer

My favourite hobby is collecting the autographs of famous people. I've got over 200 autographs at the moment, and I've collected the signatures of all sorts of famous people – sports people, actors, musicians and TV stars. I go to lots of events that famous people are attending and I wait in the best place, for example the entrance to a building – and I ask the person to sign their name in my book when they are going in or out. I love it because I can speak to famous people and then I can look at my collection and show it to other people.

I started the hobby when I was walking past a hotel in the city centre one day and a very famous pop star suddenly came out. I asked her for her autograph. She signed her name on a piece of paper and that was my first autograph. After that, I wanted to collect more autographs and it became my main hobby. Now I spend most weekends trying to get more autographs.

QUESTION 4 *Task specific mark scheme*

Content

The report should describe one or more fashions among young people in the place where the writer lives. It does not have to describe any of the fashions listed in the question because candidates are told they can describe any fashion they choose. The report must also contain the writer's opinion(s).

Range of grammar and vocabulary

The fashion must be described using the appropriate present tense(s). Appropriate vocabulary connected with the chosen fashion(s) is required, as well as appropriate structures and vocabulary for giving opinions.

Register

The report may be fairly formal or neutral if the candidate is talking about something they regard as fairly serious. On the other hand, the report may be quite informal, to entertain or amuse the reader.

Organization and cohesion

If more than one fashion is described, the report should be divided into appropriate sections, probably with a title for each section. If a single fashion is described, the report may be in the form of a single paragraph. The whole report may be given a title. Appropriate linking words and phrases should be used (e.g. *For example*

to introduce an example of young people following a particular fashion).

Target reader

The reader should understand exactly what the fashion or fashions involve (and the reader may know nothing about the fashion(s) before reading the report). The reader should also understand what the writer thinks of the fashion(s).

Model answer

FASHIONABLE PHRASES

The latest fashion among young people in the place where I live is connected with a TV programme that's very popular at the moment. The programme is called 'Bleep' and it's a drama series about the lives of various teenagers. It's supposed to be funny and the characters in it all use certain phrases all the time. People copy the phrases these characters use and they say them all the time. If you don't watch the programme, you don't know what people are talking about now. People whisper these phrases in class and then everyone laughs, or they say them to each other in the street and then they all start laughing. It's like some kind of special language that they all use now. For example, one character in the programme is always saying 'You must be mad'. People say that all the time now, even when it doesn't make sense. Personally, I think this is a pretty silly fashion. I like the programme, but I don't understand why everyone keeps saying these things and then laughing. They must be mad!

Paper 3: Use of English

PART 1

1	B	5	B	9	B
2	A	6	C	10	C
3	D	7	C	11	A
4	D	8	A	12	B

PART 2

13	which/that	17	not	21	enough
14	as	18	to	22	if/should
15	and	19	having	23	those
16	for	20	too	24	well

PART 3

25	coincidence	30	wedding(s)
26	conversation	31	birth
27	discoveries	32	exactly
28	seventies	33	engagement
29	unlikely	34	unbelievable

PART 4

35 to][the **advice** you gave
36 far as][I'm **concerned**
37 has a **tendency**][to behave
38 **twice** as][much (money) as
39 **made** me][lose my
40 so **much**][skill
41 as a **result**][of getting
42 **ran** into][a friend of

Paper 4: Listening

PART 1

1	C	4	A	7	A
2	B	5	C	8	A
3	B	6	A		

PART 2

9 domestic dogs
10 E/environmental M/management
11 corporate
12 competition prizes
13 radio presenter
14 certificate
15 more than five/5 times
16 (heated) indoor play area
17 animal keeper
18 voluntary

PART 3

19	F	22	C
20	B	23	A
21	E		

PART 4

24	C	28	B
25	C	29	A
26	B	30	C
27	A		

Paper 5: Speaking

Teachers should use their own judgement to award marks out of 20 based on the assessment criteria on page 94.

TEST 4

Paper 1: Reading

PART 1

1	D	5	B
2	A	6	C
3	C	7	D
4	D	8	A

PART 2

9	F	13	B
10	H	14	G
11	A	15	D
12	E		

PART 3

16/17	C/F	21	A	26	D
18	E	22	F	27/28	A/D
19	D	23	C	29	B
20	C	24/25	A/E	30	E

Paper 2: Writing

For General impression mark scheme see page 93.

QUESTION 1 *Task specific mark scheme*

Content

The email must include something relating to each of the notes – how the writers' friends felt about meeting Max and news about each of the friends mentioned.

Range of grammar and vocabulary

The email should include the appropriate use of tenses – present simple and/or present continuous for current situations, present perfect and/or past simple for news of the friends' activities, and future structures for future plans and activities. Vocabulary connected with the various activities should be used accurately.

Register

The email should be fairly informal because it is from one friend to another.

Organization and cohesion

The email should begin with a reference to Max's email and to the writer's friends, and this should be followed by news about each of the friends mentioned. News of each friend may be in separate paragraphs.

Target reader

The reader should understand that the friends liked him/her and should be clear about what each friend has been doing.

Model answer

Hi Max,

Thanks for the message. It was great having you here too and my friends really enjoyed meeting you and spending time with you. They often ask me about you.

Yes, Tim and Eddie have still got their band, and they're doing well. They're getting quite a lot of bookings to play at various places and in a few weeks they're going to play at a very big concert here.

Ruth did get the job in the museum and she really loves it. She's done so well that she's now in charge of a whole department, so she's very happy about that.

Richard and Anna started their travels about two months ago. The last time I got a postcard from them, they were in Africa and they were having a great time. I don't know when they're coming back.

Please write back and tell me what your news is.

QUESTION 2 *Task specific mark scheme*

Content

The review should give a brief summary of the game and the writer's opinions of it, with reasons.

Range of grammar and vocabulary

The review should use appropriate structures for describing a game, including the appropriate present tense(s) for describing what you do and appropriate modal verbs (*must, have to, can't,* etc.) for describing the rules. Appropriate structures for giving opinions should also be used. Vocabulary appropriate for the game chosen should be used accurately.

Register

The review should be neutral or informal – the factual description may be neutral and the opinions informal.

Organization and cohesion

The review should be organized appropriately into paragraphs providing factual information on the game and opinions of it.

Target reader

The reader should get a clear general idea of what the game involves and should understand what the writer thinks of the game.

Model answer

MONOPOLY

I recently played a game of Monopoly, which is one of the oldest board games in the world. You can buy different versions of it in different countries.

Basically, the game is about buying different properties that are on the board. You throw dice and move around the board and you can choose to buy properties that you land on. If you land on a property that belongs to another player, you have to pay them. Everyone gets a certain amount of money at the start, and if you have no money left, you're out of the game.

The game is quite good fun, and to be good at it you have to think about what the best strategy is. You have to think like a business person. I think it's been popular for so long because it's easy to play but also quite interesting because it's not too simple.

The only problem with Monopoly is that it can take a very long time to play the game, and so it can become quite boring.

QUESTION 3 *Task specific mark scheme*

Content

The letter should explain what the competition or tournament was, describe the writer's experience when he/she entered it, and describe the writer's feelings about the experience.

Range of grammar and vocabulary

The letter should use appropriate past tenses for describing the experience (the past simple and perhaps past continuous and past perfect tenses). Vocabulary appropriate to the sport or type of competition should be used accurately, as well as vocabulary for describing feelings.

Register

The letter may be neutral or fairly informal. It is for a magazine, not an individual that the writer knows, but the announcement is asking for personal experiences and so the letter should not be too formal.

Organization and cohesion

The letter may be divided into paragraphs, dealing with the general background, the actual experience and the writer's feelings. It should clearly describe the sequence of events. Appropriate linking should be used for each part of the sequence of events and for linking the events with the writer's feelings about them.

Target reader

The reader should understand clearly what the writer entered, what happened and how the writer felt about it or feels about it now.

Model answer

To the Editor,

Last year I entered a regional tennis tournament. I was in the under-17 age group and the tournament took place at the biggest tennis club in the area. I didn't expect to do very well in the tournament but I decided to enter and see what happened.

When I got to the club, I was quite nervous because I had never played at such a big club. When I was getting changed before my first game, all the other players seemed much more confident than me.

I won my first game and I was really pleased about that. It made me much more confident and then I won my next game too. Eventually I reached the semi-final, but I lost that game. The other player was much better than me. She won the tournament and people say she's one of the best players in the country in that age group.

After the tournament I was very proud of what I had achieved and I realized that I am a good player. I'm planning to enter more tournaments now.

Yours sincerely,

QUESTION 4 *Task specific mark scheme*

Content

The essay should fully address the point made in the statement, and not include points that are not directly relevant to that. The writer may agree or disagree or both agree and disagree. The writer does not have to conclude that he/she agrees or disagrees.

Range of grammar and vocabulary

It is likely that modal verbs (e.g. *should, can, might*, etc.) will be required to give views on what people are and are not able to do. The present simple verb tense is required to talk about general situations. Conditional structures may be required to talk about possible situations and the results of them. Vocabulary connected with work and making decisions should be used accurately.

Register

The essay may be fairly formal or neutral, as the subject is a fairly serious one.

Organization and cohesion

The essay may be divided into appropriate paragraphs, each one making separate general points. It may be organized into one paragraph of agreement with the statement and one of disagreement. Appropriate linking words and phrases should be used for linking views with reasons that support those views.

Target reader

The reader must fully understand the writer's opinions on the topic and the reasons why the writer has those opinions.

Model answer

In many countries in modern times it is not necessary to decide what kind of career you are going to have until you are older. These days lots of people change their careers many times through their lives. In the past, most people had to choose a career when they were young and then stay in that career for all of their working lives. Nowadays, it's possible to try different careers before you decide on the one you want to concentrate on. This is a good thing, because it gives people more freedom. They can decide on their career when they are older and have more experience of life. This means that they are more likely to choose a career they enjoy.

On the other hand, it is important to decide on some careers when you are still quite young, because it is harder to start those careers when you are older. If you want to be a doctor, or an architect, or have any career that requires many years of training, you need to make your decision when you are still quite young.

Paper 3: Use of English

PART 1

1	A	5	C	9	A
2	C	6	B	10	D
3	D	7	A	11	B
4	A	8	C	12	C

PART 2

13	which	19	this/that
14	between	20	is
15	for	21	than
16	all	22	being
17	any	23	as
18	be	24	so

PART 3

25	invitations/invites	30	technique
26	dislike	31	ensures
27	advice	32	legendary
28	listeners	33	shortly
29	attention	34	Unfortunately

PART 4

35 we're/we are **supposed**][to reply
36 must have][**left** it
37 it took (me)][**longer** than
38 to **catch**][on
39 at the **time**][of
40 of][at **least**
41 doesn't/does not **know**][how to
42 made][**a note** of

Paper 4: Listening

PART 1

1	C	5	B
2	B	6	A
3	C	7	B
4	B	8	A

PART 2

9	loan	14	socially responsible
10	an engineer	15	multiple entries
11	poorest people	16	script
12	one/1 minute	17	passion
13	product; service	18	ten/10

PART 3

19	E	22	B
20	C	23	D
21	A		

PART 4

24	A	28	B
25	C	29	B
26	A	30	C
27	A		

Paper 5: Speaking

Teachers should use their own judgement to award marks
out of 20 based on the assessment criteria on page 94.

TEST 1

Part One.
You will hear people talking in eight different situations.
For questions 1–8, choose the best answer, A, B or C.

ONE.
You hear someone talking about football referees.
What is the speaker's attitude towards referees?
A They make too many mistakes.
B They deserve sympathy.
C Some are better than others.

Man: You have to feel sorry for referees. I mean, they're under terrible pressure throughout the game, with players shouting at them, and cheating and all that. And of course, the fans of both sides give them a hard time – they just can't win. Sure, they make mistakes, plenty of them, but they're only human. They don't go out there thinking, 'I'm going to do really badly today,' they're doing their best. Some people think that there are referees who just want to draw attention to themselves, who think they're as important as the players, but that's not my view. I mean, who'd want their job, with all that criticism all the time? *repeat extract 1*

TWO.
You hear a famous chef talking about his week. What does he say about what happened during the week?
A He had a problem that was not his fault.
B He didn't want to appear on so many programmes.
C He had his first experience of live TV.

Chef: I had a bit of an odd week. I went to Birmingham to do a TV cookery show. I had to make my special recipe pancakes, but the pan they gave me in the studio wasn't nearly big enough, so it made things all a bit difficult. But it turned out all right in the end, they were just a bit smaller than usual! Later in the week I was on a radio show answering listeners' questions about cooking, and then I did a few interviews about my new book. *repeat extract 2*

THREE.
You hear someone talking about her career in dancing. What does she emphasize?
A the contribution made by her parents
B how much hard work she did
C her desire to be a dancer

Woman: I just had to dance. When I was a girl, I was always putting on dancing shows for my parents. By the time I was seven I knew what I wanted to be, and that feeling never went away. I told my parents I wanted to do proper ballet. So I went to a ballet school and I've been dancing ever since. I used to have classes after school and on Saturdays. And, when I finished school, I went to a full-time dance academy for four years. Now I'm teaching dance, and I've never been happier.

repeat extract 3

FOUR.
You hear someone talking on the phone at work. Who is she talking to?
A a colleague
B her boss
C a client

Woman: So what time are you going to make it? You know it's a very important meeting and we can't really discuss the issue properly without you. Yes, I'll tell her you'll get here as soon as you can, but I know she isn't going to be very pleased. OK, I'll delay things as long as I can – I'll say you've got problems at home or something. No, I won't say you've overslept, I don't want to get you in trouble. *repeat extract 4*

FIVE.
You hear a radio presenter talking about a book. What feeling does the presenter express about the book?
A doubt that it does exactly what it says it does
B amazement at how up to date its information is
C curiosity about how it was written

Presenter: Have you ever wondered how many tons of food you eat in a lifetime, or how many miles of blood vessels there are in your body? No? Oh well, there are plenty more intriguing entries in this huge book of facts. It claims to have the most accurate and up-to-date information about every subject on Earth. I'm not sure it covers absolutely everything, but it certainly has lots of fascinating facts on pretty much any topic you can think of – you won't be able to put it down!

repeat extract 5

SIX.
You hear part of an interview with a famous comedian. What does he say about his school days?
A The teachers never criticized him.
B He was only good at one subject.
C Other people found him amusing.

Interviewer: What was your favourite subject at school?
Man: Maths, by far. I loved it, so I was good at it. I couldn't get enthusiastic about other subjects, but with maths I wanted to show off. I liked the logic of it.
Interviewer: Were you a good student?
Man: Yes, pretty much. I didn't cause a lot of trouble or anything like that. I was cheeky and I liked having a laugh with my friends, but I always managed to make the teachers laugh before they told me off. All in all, I had a great time at school. *repeat extract 6*

SEVEN.

You hear someone talking about a person he knows. What is the speaker doing?

A complaining
B apologizing
C arguing

Man: I really don't see why I have to keep doing him favours. He never does any for me. I guess you were right about him all along – you always said he took advantage of other people. I didn't believe you then but now I can see what you mean. I can see now that I was totally wrong about him. It's a real shame, because I thought we were great friends for a while. But I'm just not going to put up with him any longer. I mean, he surely can't expect to behave like that and get away with it. *repeat extract 7*

EIGHT.

You hear a tour guide talking to a group of visitors to a museum. What does he tell them about the museum?

A It's easy to get lost in it.
B Big groups aren't allowed in some parts of it.
C It's better only to visit a small part of it.

Guide: OK, that's the end of my introductory talk and now you can wander around on your own for a couple of hours. We'll meet back here at 12.30. Before you go, a bit of advice. This is an enormous museum, packed full of fascinating things, and you can't expect to see it all in one go. So, if I were you I'd concentrate on one or two sections and look at them in detail. Have a look at the map – you've all got one and it's very simple and clear – and decide where you want to go. And split up into couples or small groups – it gets pretty crowded here and you won't have much fun if a lot of you try to stick together. *repeat extract 8*

That is the end of Part One. Now turn to Part Two.

You will hear someone talking about the sport of elephant polo. For questions 9–18, complete the sentences. You now have 45 seconds to look at Part 2.

Elephant polo player: Of course, polo is normally played on horses, and it's a very fast game. Well, we don't claim that elephant polo is the fastest game in the world, but we always maintain it's the biggest. The elephants do actually enjoy polo. Definitely. It's a lot of fun for them because they're social animals, and a polo tournament is a week when dozens of elephants meet up, many from the same family, like a reunion. And of course they get fed extremely well – better than in their normal life. They use up a lot of energy and get through masses of sugar cane, especially at half-time.

The players sit on elephants and hit a white wooden ball, using a long bamboo stick that has a polo mallet head on the end of it. The pitch is about three-quarters the length of a football pitch, and the goals are the same width as football goals. There's a basic saddle and the players are strapped onto the elephants. We've never had a serious accident. A mahout – an elephant handler – sits behind each player and guides the elephant. Sometimes the mahouts have their own games, guiding the elephant and hitting the ball as well. That takes incredible skill.

During a game, if the ball hits an elephant, that's fine. Their legs are quite thick and they do get in the way. Quite often they will kick the ball so that they can run after it. They're not allowed to pick up the ball with their trunks, though they sometimes try. That would be a free hit to the other side.

There are four elephants per team in a tournament, plus the referee's elephant – that's nine on the pitch at any one time. We usually have sixteen animals available on any given day, in four teams. There are two halves, called chukkas, in a game of elephant polo, the same as in normal polo. We play ten minutes of actual play. Whenever the whistle blows, the clock stops. A novice team might score one or two goals, if they're lucky, while an advanced team might score about ten.

The polo rules are that a man can only hold the stick with his right arm, even if he is left-handed. Women can use both hands. Using the stick is hard work, because it's long and the head is heavy. By the end of the game, your arm will be aching. But it's an easy game to pick up with a little practice.

During the game, you chase after the ball on your elephant, going quite quickly, and you can easily miss it, though the elephant will often help you out with his foot. The elephants usually supply the entertainment. They might decide to lie down across the goal for fun but that's an absolute no-no.

Ultimately it's about elephants charging up and down the pitch, scoring great goals themselves and having a lot of fun. If the elephants didn't enjoy it, or if there was any form of misbehaving, they would be removed from the game – sent off, if you like. It's not worth risking an elephant with an attitude problem.

You get all sorts. You get big elephants that are a bit older and wiser, and we use a lot of small ones that can be exceptionally quick. We try to remove what you might call the elephant factor by swapping elephants and mahouts with the other team at half-time. If you've got elephants that don't normally live together, there can be some tension. The sport always uses Indian elephants. The problem with African ones is that their ears get in the way. And they're much taller.

In the exam you will hear the recording twice. To listen again now, go to the beginning of the track.

That is the end of Part Two. Now turn to Part Three.

You will hear five different people talking about cities they have visited. For questions 19–23, choose from the list A–F the opinion each person gives about the city. Use the letters only once. There is one extra letter which you do not need to use. You now have 30 seconds to look at Part Three.

Speaker 1: The place is always on TV and in films and in magazines, and so you get a mental picture of what it's like even if you haven't been there. You have this image of skyscrapers everywhere, streets full of traffic and people, everyone rushing around, talking fast and leading busy lives. You think of it as having a real buzz. And guess what? It was just like that. Everything I'd expected to find was there. In fact, it all seemed so familiar that it was as if I'd actually been there before.

Speaker 2: I discovered after I'd been there that you need to be really careful about when you choose to visit the place. There are very busy times and quieter times. Without realizing it, I chose one of the busy times, and wow, was it busy! The place was packed, and of course with the narrow streets it is famed for, that makes movement difficult. I just shuffled along with everyone else, going at their pace, so I didn't manage to see much. There's a great atmosphere there, and of course it looks wonderful, but I could have done with a bit more room to move. So I guess I didn't see it at its best.

Speaker 3: Everyone I've met who's been there says what a fantastic place it is, and I was expecting something really special. And I wasn't disappointed, though I must say the picture I'd had of it in my mind didn't turn out to be totally accurate. In fact, it not only lived up to my expectations, it exceeded them. People always associate it with its famous buildings, but it was the less well-known places that struck me. In every little street, especially away from the tourist areas, there was something fascinating to see. It's those little streets that were really memorable for me.

Speaker 4: I'd been looking forward to going there for a long time and I finally managed it. I wasn't quite sure what to expect because people had told me that it wasn't the same as it used to be. Apparently, it's become much more touristy recently, but I didn't see any evidence of that. What did strike me was how confusing it is. Half the time I didn't know where I was and getting from A to B was always problematic. I normally have a good sense of direction, but I was always getting lost there. Once I did get to where I was trying to go, it was worth it, though.

Speaker 5: People always talk about what a marvellous place it is, and so eventually I decided to go and see for myself. It has the reputation of being a place you never forget, and lots of people say it's their favourite city. But, having been there, I can't see what all the fuss is about. Sure, the places that you see pictures of all the time, or that you see in films, are impressive enough, but I've seen better. It's a pleasant enough place, and it's certainly popular with tourists – there were plenty of them there – but I don't think it really deserves all the praise people give it.

In the exam you will hear the recording twice. To listen again now, go to the beginning of the track.

That is the end of Part Three. Now turn to Part Four.

You will hear an interview with someone who is involved in the music business. For questions 24–30, choose the best answer, A, B or C. You now have one minute to look at Part Four.

Interviewer: My next guest is James Hyland, the young Irish entrepreneur, who has been behind all sorts of music projects. The latest is Bubble TV, a music channel without advertising breaks. James, welcome.

James: Hi.

Interviewer: You're 23 now, but you launched yourself into the music world while you were still at school, didn't you? You were a very young starter!

James: Yes, I was 12 when I started my own radio station in my house. I played music I liked. The station was called Happiness. Not a good name I know, but I was young. I would have been happy if it had been just the neighbours listening, but it soon became clear that I'd attracted a lot of fans and I was invited to play at events. I ploughed all the money I made from that back into the station. It got very big and I got noticed.

Interviewer: Weren't people amazed when they found out you were 12?

James: Yes, but they were far more amazed when they discovered that I was organizing concerts by some of the biggest bands on the British music scene when I was just 16. That also attracted a lot of jealous rivalry. At 12 people are pleased for you, people are happy and encourage you, but when you're just a little older and running a successful business, it can be more of a threat.

Interviewer: So how did your career in music progress as you got older?

James: When I was 16, I started working with a local radio station. I didn't stay too long as I didn't like having a boss. But I didn't just complain and carry on going into work. I ditched the job and set up my own studio at my home in Cork, in southern Ireland, and began producing commercials from there. Along the way, I'd already started promoting well-known bands. I managed to bring in some fantastic acts to play at festivals and concerts in Ireland.

Interviewer: Now not so long ago, you launched the Bubble TV channel, a 24-hour all-music channel with no advertising breaks, aimed at teenagers. James, you seem to be the sort of person who's too busy to be the couch potato type, but the idea came from watching TV, didn't it?

James: Yes, I was flicking through all the channels and noticed there were so many of them but only three dedicated to music. And there weren't any exclusively British channels – most were from the US with British commercials. I hate ad breaks, they interrupt whatever you're watching and spoil the mood, so I decided not to have any. However, I should point out that Bubble TV has sponsored segments, so companies are involved. But the sponsorship doesn't get in the way, you have to look for a change in the background logo during programmes to notice it.

Interviewer: Is it just music and nothing else?

James: Although it's mainly music, we have three presenters, who do slots called Juice. They interview bands and go to gigs and festivals. And bands can't just promote their new song or whatever, it's got to be fun. They have to spill the juice – the gossip – in just three-minute slots! It has to be entertaining.

Interviewer: Now, you're constantly coming up with fresh ideas. Do you sleep with a notebook by the bed in case you dream up a best-selling idea in your sleep?

James: Absolutely. I text myself with my ideas as I have them, then each day I go through my texts to see what ideas I have sent myself.

Interviewer: So what's next?

James: Aah, I have several ideas ... but I'm not telling you!

Interviewer: OK, fair enough! Well, finally, have you got any tips for would-be entrepreneurs listening now?

James: Don't give up at the first sign of hardship. I've had my fingers burnt and lost money through some of my schemes in the past, but I've never let it get me down. I've had setbacks – but you can't dwell on them. You just move on.

Interviewer: James, thanks.

James: You're welcome.

In the exam you will hear the recording twice. To listen again now, go to the beginning of the track.

That is the end of Part Four.

TEST 2

Part One.
You will hear people talking in eight different situations.
For questions 1–8, choose the best answer, A, B or C.

ONE.
You hear part of an interview with a sportsman. What does he say about playing for the national team?
A He doesn't think it will happen soon.
B It isn't his main concern at the moment.
C The possibility of it happening has put him under pressure.

Interviewer: There's been talk of you being picked for the national team again. Is it hard for you to put that to the back of your mind during games, when you know that the national coach could be watching?

Sportsman: Playing for your country is as big as it gets, and it'd be great to do that again. But at the same time you have to worry about the job on the day, and that's playing for your club. I've learned over the years that your focus should be on the game you're playing in and nothing else. *repeat extract 1*

TWO.
You hear the introduction to a radio programme. What is the speaker doing?
A contrasting weather forecasting in the past and the present
B explaining why weather forecasting has become more accurate
C joking about how people used to forecast the weather

Presenter: Now, what do you do if you want to know what the weather is going to be like? You probably turn on the television or look on the Internet. But meteorology is a relatively recent science, and not so long ago people, especially farmers, had to rely on their own knowledge of the seasons. And no season was more important than spring. Many different rhymes and sayings were used for predicting the weather, and each month had its own sayings. *repeat extract 2*

THREE.
You hear a man talking about reading aloud to children. What opinion does he express?
A Short stories are better than longer books.
B The choice of book may not be important.
C It's hard to know what will make children laugh.

Man: It doesn't really matter what you read to kids, they appreciate anything. I've been reading a book about history to my seven-year-old. He doesn't understand a word of it, but insists on having it every night. Having said that, it does make a huge difference if you can find a book that you all enjoy together. My favourite is a series of short stories about a mad inventor who creates ridiculous machines. It's great to be able to read something that genuinely makes your children laugh. *repeat extract 3*

FOUR.
You hear someone talking about work. What is his situation?
A He has just left a job.
B He is thinking of leaving his job.
C He has just started a new job.

Man: So that's it. After all the months of worrying about it and discussing it with other people, I've finally done it. To be honest, I'm not sure how I feel. A bit anxious about the future, sure, because I really don't know how things are going to go. But I simply had to get out. You can't go on putting up with the sort of things I had to put up with. I still can't help thinking that it shouldn't have come to this. But it did, and I've dealt with it and it's time now to start looking ahead. *repeat extract 4*

FIVE.

You hear someone talking about his childhood. What does he mention?

A a habit he regards as strange
B regret about some of his behaviour
C how much he has changed

Man: When I was a kid, I was always jumping out of windows and things and climbing trees. I had numerous injuries from things like that. Also, I went through a phase of wearing all my clothes back to front. Even to this day I don't know why I did it. In fact, I occasionally still do. I put my clothes on back to front and just sit there on my own because it reminds me of when I was a kid. *repeat extract 5*

SIX.

You hear someone talking about something that happened at a party. How did the speaker feel?

A upset
B amused
C frightened

Man: Yes, it was completely unexpected. I had no idea he felt so strongly about it. I mean, as far as I'm concerned I just made an innocent comment and he suddenly went mad. He was shouting at me and pointing his finger and I thought at one point he might even get violent. How silly. He just succeeded in making a complete fool of himself. Everyone else was looking terribly worried but I thought it was all highly entertaining. Some of those insults he was shouting at me – so ridiculous. I expect he'll apologize eventually but I really don't care. *repeat extract 6*

SEVEN.

You hear part of a talk about blues music. What is the speaker talking about?

A why it originated in a certain area
B how popular it was in the past compared with today
C its importance in the history of popular music

Woman: Of course, without blues, you simply wouldn't have any of the various forms of popular music that have swept the world over the past few decades. Rock'n'roll, soul, rap, hip-hop – they all owe their existence to the style of music that was created in a small part of the Deep South of the US – the Mississippi Delta. The musicians who developed the style were all more or less totally unknown outside their own area, although fortunately they made plenty of recordings

that are still available today if you want to find out more. And you should, if you want to find out where a lot of today's music came from. *repeat extract 7*

EIGHT.

You hear someone on the radio talking about a website for consumers. What is the speaker's purpose?

A to encourage consumers to make complaints
B to inform consumers about a source of information
C to describe common problems for consumers

Man: This is the first place to go if you need information about your rights as a consumer. It has tips on dealing with dodgy workmen, faulty goods, shopping safely online and avoiding scams. It's relatively easy to navigate your way around it, has a useful links section and will help you get in touch with telephone advisers. It will not, however, take up individual cases. *repeat extract 8*

That is the end of Part One. Now turn to Part Two.

You will hear a radio interview about indoor skydiving. For questions 9–18, complete the sentences. You now have 45 seconds to look at Part 2.

Presenter: OK, now we come to our regular spot on extreme sports, and this week our fearless reporter Tom Walker has been trying out something called indoor skydiving. And he's with me now. Tom, what's this all about?

Reporter: Well, it's the same as skydiving – jumping from an aeroplane and freefalling through the air without opening your parachute for some time – except that you do it in an indoor wind tunnel. And there's no plane, and no parachute, and, so I was told, no danger! So it gives you a taste of doing an extreme sport, but it isn't quite so extreme.

Presenter: Right, now where did you do it?

Reporter: I did it in a vertical wind tunnel at an adventure sports centre called Runway.

Presenter: What exactly is a vertical wind tunnel?

Reporter: Well, it's a tunnel that gets filled with air. The air is provided by four enormous industrial fans of a kind that usually provide air for underground systems. These fans produce a column of air that rushes through the tunnel from below at more than 160 kilometres per hour. When you're in the tunnel, you float on this air. The machine has been described as being like an enormous hairdryer. It allows you to fly as if you had fallen from a plane, but you are only two metres off the ground.

Presenter: And it's completely safe is it?

Reporter: Yes. There are bars across the top of the tunnel to stop you flying off up and out of the tunnel. The tunnel is four metres wide and has glass walls. The only small problem you might have is that you keep bashing into these walls. But you're not really going to hurt yourself a lot by doing this – the only injuries you are likely to get are sore elbows and knees. In fact, it's so safe that the centre is open to anyone over the age of four. In America, where the idea was invented by the military in 1994, pensioners in their eighties regularly have a go.

Presenter: Wow! So how did you get on when you went there?

Reporter: Well, when I got there I watched the training instructors running through their routine. They were doing all sorts of moves in the tunnel, such as 'barrel rolls', something they call 'helicopters' – spinning on their heads in mid-air, and back flips. Watching them do all that before I went into the tunnel left me feeling a little anxious, even though I knew the tunnel was safe. And the roar of the electric motors that power the fans, like a plane taking off and so loud you need ear-plugs, added to my fear.

Presenter: What happened when you went into the tunnel?

Reporter: Like all beginners, I was given a couple of two-minute sessions in the tunnel, which seems short, but since the average freefall from a plane lasts only one minute, you realize it is more than plenty. Held down by my instructor, I floated in the position I was told to keep to, with my hands out in front of me as if I was 'holding a ball of air', for the whole session. The only time he had to correct me was on the occasions I threatened to fly out of reach or, as if by instinct, disappear out of the entry-exit door.

Presenter: Sounds exciting.

Reporter: Yeah, it's great fun. In fact the person who came up with the idea and set up the centre calls it a 'smile machine', because nobody can go into the tunnel without smiling.

Presenter: So you recommend it?

Reporter: Yes, it's just like real skydiving, except that you don't have the view – or the expense! And it's good both for beginners and extreme skydivers. In fact, in some places it has developed into its own sport, known as body flying. There are already competitions in that sport.

Presenter: Thanks, Tom, If you want to find out more about the wind tunnel, ... (fade)

In the exam you will hear the recording twice. To listen again now, go to the beginning of the track.

That is the end of Part Two. Now turn to Part Three.

You will hear five different people talking about the reasons why they became very successful. For questions 19–23, choose from the list A–F the reason each person gives for their success. Use the letters only once. There is one extra letter which you do not need to use. You now have thirty seconds to look at Part Three.

Speaker 1: I just fell into my television career really, there was no grand scheme. I guess it was all a case of simply being in the right place at the right time. I got my first job by pure chance and then one job offer followed another. I didn't set out to get where I am today and I'm sure there are plenty of people who could do the job as well as, if not better than, me. People tell me they like what I do, and that's great, but I'd probably be just as happy if the whole thing hadn't happened.

Speaker 2: When I started the company, the market was wide open really and hardly anyone was doing what I was doing. Actually, the product I was offering in the early days wasn't all that good, but there wasn't much to compare it with, so it did OK. The fact is, it was a good idea and in business there's no substitute for a good idea. I'm not necessarily a brilliant businessman in terms of strategy and things like that and sometimes I'm not sure what to do next. But I did have that great idea, so I've made my own luck.

Speaker 3: My personal feeling is that in show business, talent will always get its reward. Even if you have to struggle on for years – which, thankfully I didn't have to do – if you've got what it takes, you'll make it. Someone will spot you and give you a part if you're good enough, and that's exactly what happened to me. I've never really had to work at it, it just seems to be something I was born with. I've never thought of doing anything else, and fortunately I've never had to.

Speaker 4: There was no shortage of advice when I started my career as a singer. People told me how I should look, what sort of songs I should sing, all sorts of things. But I ignored them all, and I'm glad I did because I've been proved right. I had it all worked out from the very beginning, every detail of what I was going to do and how I was going to do it and it's all gone very smoothly. I knew what suited me and what would be popular and I've followed my instincts on that. I haven't had to struggle at all, everything's gone very well.

Speaker 5: To get to the top in my sport I've had to make the most of what I've got. I may not be the most talented player there's ever been but I've put a tremendous amount of effort in to be as good as I can be. All along there have been people making comments about how I'm not good enough, but that's just made me try even harder. And I've exceeded my ambitions really – I only wanted to be a good club player and I never imagined I'd make it into the national side.

In the exam you will hear the recording twice. To listen again now, go to the beginning of the track.

That is the end of Part Three. Now turn to Part Four.

You will hear someone giving a talk about taking up running as an activity. For questions 24–30, choose the best answer, A, B or C. You now have one minute to look at Part Four.

Speaker: As someone who didn't even own a pair of running shoes until I was in my twenties, I think I'm well placed to talk about the virtues of taking up running. After a childhood and youth spent – or misspent – avoiding physical activity and sport at all costs, I am now, a decade and a half on, fitter and healthier than ever, and have completed more than 100 races, including ten marathons. Through my running I have gained a wonderful sense of independence, greater confidence, discipline and focus, a sanctuary from daily stresses and some great friendships. I can't quite remember what it was that first motivated me to go huffing and puffing my way around the block – but whatever it was, I'm thankful for it now. And that's why I am so keen to persuade you to do the same.

You'll find that no other exercise variety gets results as fast as running. Give it a go and I promise you three things. Firstly, every muscle from the waist down will become stronger, tighter and firmer while excess body fat will be sent marching. Secondly, you'll feel great about yourself. You'll have more energy, you'll feel alert and focused and you'll experience a real sense of accomplishment as you gradually become fitter and stronger. Finally, you'll find that running is very easy to fit into your life. Unlike that exercise class, you don't have to be somewhere dead on six o'clock, unlike swimming you don't have to get to the pool before closing time, unlike tennis or squash, you don't have to rely on someone else to make it happen. You can go for fifteen minutes at lunchtime, or grab half an hour in the morning. You can hit the city streets or head for the park. All in all you can make running fit into your life without too much effort. And when you do, you'll be helping yourself not only to a healthier life, but a longer and happier one, too.

Is that a 'but' I can hear? 'But I'm too old/overweight/ embarrassed …, etc.'. These are worries that people often reveal when they are faced with the prospect of taking up exercise. Well, I can't categorically say to each and every one of you 'no, you're not' but I can tell you that I know people who have become runners in their 40s, 50s and 60s, and only wish they'd done it sooner. I know people who've gone out running in the streets in bad weather and risked funny looks from passers-by, in order to give running a go, and now wouldn't give it up for the world. After all, one of the greatest pleasures in life is overcoming fears and obstacles.

There is one warning, though. To reap these benefits, you have to approach running with patience and respect. Try to achieve too much too soon and you'll end up aching, disillusioned and possibly even injured. The golden rule is to start slow, and progress one step at a time. Some people improve quicker than others, too, so don't compare your progress to anyone else's.

Now we come to technique. If you remember only one thing about running technique when you're out there, remember to relax! It's impossible to run if you aren't relaxed. Unclench your fists, relax your jaw, keep your shoulders loose. Think 'up' before moving forwards. This helps you stay light on your feet, and makes you run tall rather than sinking into the hips. Remember to use your arms. Picture them as pistons, propelling you forwards. Keep them bent to roughly 90 degrees. It's particularly important to think about your arms if you hit an incline – increasing the arm effort will help you get up the hill easier. What about breathing? Always a good idea, I find! Despite all the weird and wonderful theories about breathing in through your nose and out through your mouth, or breathing in time with your footfall, I recommend just getting the oxygen in whatever way feels most comfortable to you.

Now, I'm going to give you the details of the Get Running programme. This provides an 8-week schedule …

In the exam you will hear the recording twice. To listen again now, go to the beginning of the track.

That is the end of Part Four.

TEST 3

Part One
You will hear people talking in eight different situations. For questions 1–8, choose the best answer, A, B or C.

ONE.
You hear part of an interview with a pop singer. How does she feel about what happened?
A embarrassed by her mistake
B angry with her tour manager
C confused about what happened

Interviewer: I hear that you missed a concert you were supposed to do in Germany recently. How did that happen?
Female singer: Well, I just lost my passport. I couldn't find it anywhere in my house. Obviously, I would say that it wasn't my fault, but, well, it wasn't my fault! I just assumed that our tour manager had it. But he didn't have it. He normally keeps it for me when I'm travelling for concerts and I don't know how it got lost. I've had to get a replacement one. *repeat extract 1*

TWO.
You hear part of a radio programme for young people. What advice does the speaker give?
A Try to discuss the matter with your friends.
B Pay no attention to the people who laugh at you.
C Encourage other people to be like you.

Woman: We've got an email from Beth, who says, 'My family hasn't got a car, and we walk or cycle everywhere. My friends laugh at me because they all have cars. What should I do?' Well, Beth, there is a lot to be said for not having a car unless you really need one. In fact, it would be much better for the environment if fewer people had cars. Your so-called friends are unkind to judge you on what you have or don't have. People like this are very materialistic and not worth bothering with. And think how much fitter and healthier than them you'll be because of all the exercise you get! *repeat extract 2*

THREE.

You hear a radio presenter talking about a book. What does the presenter say about the book?

A   Some of the writers have already had their work published.

B   It contains work that was entered for a competition.

C   It is very well organized.

Presenter: The country's most talented young writers have seen their hard work come to fruition with the publication of the very first Young Writer's Year Book. Thousands of children aged nine to seventeen submitted their stories and poems to win a chance to be published. The successful entries have now been published in this wonderful book. Sad, surprising, witty, frightening, insightful, wise and full of potential, this is a deliciously fresh collection by the best-selling authors of the future. *repeat extract 3*

FOUR.

You hear someone talking on the phone. What is the speaker's purpose?

A   to resolve a disagreement

B   to make a threat

C   to apologize for previous behaviour

Man: Look, I don't see why this has to become a big thing. The fact is that our ideas aren't that far apart and I'm sure if we just have a reasonable chat about the situation, we can sort things out. What do you think? I mean, it makes no sense to have a big row about it, and I know that neither of us wants to do that. I'm sure we can work something out that suits both of us, so let's do it now. I'm willing to compromise if you are. *repeat extract 4*

FIVE.

You hear someone talking to an assistant at a box office. What is the situation?

A   The man has lost his tickets.

B   The man was sent the wrong tickets.

C   The man wants to return the tickets.

Man: I know it's very late but I really would appreciate it if you could help me out. You see, something's come up at the last minute and we won't be able to make it tonight. Of course, I've already paid for the tickets and I ordered the best seats. I was looking forward to it so I'm annoyed that I'm going to have to miss the show. I know you've got your rules about not giving refunds but couldn't you make an exception for me? *repeat extract 5*

SIX.

You hear someone talking about her personality. What is the speaker doing?

A   admitting something

B   explaining something

C   promising something

Woman: I just don't seem to have any patience. I know it's not a great thing, and I really ought to be able to stay calm more instead of losing my temper, but I just can't help myself. When someone gets on my nerves I just have to tell them, it just comes straight out of my mouth. There's no excuse for it, I know I ought to have more self-control. And sometimes I do try, honestly, but it just never seems to work. *repeat extract 6*

SEVEN.

You hear two people talking. What is the relationship between them?

A   They are members of the same club.

B   They live in the same building.

C   They are studying on the same course.

Man: I haven't seen you for a while.

Woman: No, I've been really busy. I've had a couple of assignments I had to do for college and they've taken up all my time.

Man: Oh, we don't have those.

Woman: Well, I've done them now, so I've got a bit more time. Do you fancy a game some time?

Man: Sure. I'll book a court for us. How about tomorrow evening?

Woman: Sounds good. Actually, that reminds me that I have to renew my membership. I'll do it while I'm there tomorrow.

Man: Yes, I did it last month. Shall I pick you up at home?

Woman: That'd be great.

Man: OK, I'll come round for you at about 7.

Woman: Excellent. *repeat extract 7*

EIGHT.

You hear a local radio presenter talking about a competition. Which of the following is true of the competition?

A   The first part does not involve any cooking.

B   The second part involves ten people cooking on their own.

C   The final part takes place at a different restaurant.

Presenter: OK, here are the details of our competition to find the best amateur chef in the region. To enter, you have to send in a main course and dessert recipe with ingredients that cost less than £10 per person.

From the recipes sent in, we'll draw up a shortlist of ten finalists, and they'll be asked to come along to Pandora's Restaurant and cook their recipes for the panel of judges and paying customers, with the assistance of the restaurant's chef. The judges will then choose three people to go forward to the final. The final three will be asked to create a three-course recipe and cook it at the restaurant for the judges and paying customers. The judges will then choose the winner. *repeat extract 8*

That is the end of Part One.

Now turn to Part Two.

You will hear an interview with a representative of a wildlife park called Paradise Wildlife Park. For questions 9–18, complete the sentences. You now have 45 seconds to look at Part 2.

Interviewer: OK, now I understand that the Park is involved in one or two projects at the moment.

Wildlife park representative: That's right. Since 1994, we've been working with various partners to raise money and help co-ordinate something called Project Life Lion. This project involves sending teams to villages which border the Serengeti National Park in East Africa to vaccinate domestic dogs against canine distemper virus (CDV) and rabies. In 1994 over one third of the Serengeti lions died as a result of CDV, which had passed from domestic dogs to the wild animal population. In addition to that, we are currently taking part in the Atlantic Rainforest Project and supporting the Community Conservation Project.

Interviewer: So you're obviously concerned about environmental issues.

Wildlife park representative: Yes, the Park continuously monitors its environmental impact. To do that, we have our own independently-written Environmental Management System, which is now being used as a model by other organizations across the UK so that they can establish their own.

Interviewer: Now, apart from the day-to-day business of visitors to the Park, you also put on events, don't you?

Wildlife park representative: Yes, the Park is a venue for all manner of corporate events, such as product launches, team-building, special events, barbecues – the list is endless. And we play host to many charity and fund-raising events each year. For them, we are happy to help with discounted tickets and competition prizes.

Interviewer: Now, tell me about the Centre for Television and Radio Training. I gather you're connected with that.

Wildlife park representative: Yes, it's our sister company. If you've always dreamed of being a radio presenter, we offer you the opportunity to take the first steps. The Centre has a range of courses from a one-day experience to a five-day full-time course which leads to your own two-hour show on our own station, Paradise FM. The courses take place at our studio complex.

Interviewer: Wow, that sounds great. Now, back to animals, which is after all what the Park is really all about. One thing that I see you run is something called Adopt an Animal. Tell me about that.

Wildlife park representative: Yes, adopting an animal is a great way to mark a special occasion, for yourself or for a friend or loved one. All our animals are available for adoption, and to ensure that they're all affordable, whatever their size, adoptions are available in shared units of £50 and last for 12 months. If you adopt an animal, you receive a certificate, a photograph of and information about your chosen animal, and a complimentary ticket for two people to the Park.

Interviewer: Now, talking of tickets, people can get season tickets for the Park, can't they?

Wildlife park representative: That's right. Our season tickets are very popular and extremely good value for money. If you visit us more than five times during the year, you will be saving money. Season tickets are valid for 12 months and allow unlimited access to the Park. And we can even take people's passport-sized photographs for them for the season ticket – free of charge.

Interviewer: But are you open all year?

Wildlife park representative: Yes, we're open 365 days a year. With our heated indoor play area, there is still lots of fun to be had even when the weather is a bit chilly.

Interviewer: Now people can also take part in what you call Experience Days, can't they?

Wildlife park representative: Yes, the Experience Days are great to give someone who is 12 or over as a gift. One of them is called Feed the Big Cats, and gives people the opportunity to hand-feed the big cats for half an hour. Another is called Walk With Our Wolves, during which people take a walk in the woods with these impressive animals. And the other is called Shadow a Keeper, and gives people a chance to become an animal keeper for a full day.

Interviewer: Finally, if I wanted to work in the Park, what chance would I have?

Wildlife park representative: Pretty good, right now! We have a number of jobs available for enthusiastic people who are interested in customer-service work, and we employ people from the ages of 16 to 60. And we also welcome applications from adults seeking voluntary work.

Interviewer: I might apply. Thanks for talking to me today.

Wildlife park representative: You're welcome.

In the exam you will hear the recording twice. To listen again now, go to the beginning of the track.

That is the end of Part Two. Now turn to Part Three.

You will hear five different people talking about what they discovered when they read autobiographies by famous people. For questions 19–23, choose from the list A–F what each person says that they discovered. Use the letters only once. There is one extra letter which you do not need to use. You now have 30 seconds to look at Part Three.

Speaker 1: What struck me most was just how arrogant the man is! I mean, he's a fine actor and I really like everything he's been in – that's why I bought the book. But that doesn't mean that his opinions on politics and the world really matter. He seems to think they do, and that because he's been in a few successful films, people should listen to his views on everything and take them seriously. Actually, he talks a lot of rubbish about all that and that really irritated me. I wanted to read about his early life and struggles, how he got to the top and all that, but he hardly mentions that, or anything about his private life. It's really put me off him.

Speaker 2: I got the book because a friend recommended it, not because I was particularly interested in the man. In fact, from his public image on TV, I thought he was a ghastly person. Self-important, fiercely ambitious and not at all likeable is how he appears to me. So I was very surprised to find that he isn't actually like that at all, that's just for public consumption. In reality, he's a decent person who puts family and friendship first and he comes across as the sort of person you could have a pleasant chat with. He's certainly gone up in my estimation.

Speaker 3: His family seem to have played a very important part in his career, and he talks about how much help they gave him in the early days, paying for coaches and taking him to tournaments all over the place. But he admits that after he made it to the top, he didn't treat them at all well. He talks about how much pressure he was under once he became a champion and how he struggled to deal with all the attention from the media and fans. We always saw him smiling in victory, but he says that he was really horrible to the people who were closest to him. It just shows that appearances can be deceptive.

Speaker 4: Of course, people always say that comedians are actually very sad people but that doesn't seem to be the case here. With him it seems to be very much 'what you see is what you get'. The book's full of really funny stories, and he makes fun of everything, from some of the things that happened during his childhood to the big issues in the world today. He seems to have come from a very peculiar family and his descriptions of them are really amusing. You get the impression that there is no difference between his personality on stage and on screen and what he's like when he's not performing.

Speaker 5: It's quite an uplifting story, really, a real 'rags to riches' one. Of course I knew all about his enormous success as a businessman, but I didn't know anything about his background. It certainly wasn't a privileged one, and he seems to have grown up in poverty with a family who didn't really care about him at all. The way he describes his childhood, it's hard to imagine how it could have been any worse. So the fact that he managed to go from that to such incredible success and wealth makes for a really interesting story. You don't get much of an idea of the real person, but the story is great.

In the exam you will hear the recording twice. To listen again now, go to the beginning of the track.

That is the end of Part Three. Now turn to Part Four.

You will hear an interview with someone whose daughters are appearing in a show in London. For questions 24–30, choose the best answer, A, B or C. You now have one minute to look at Part Four.

Interviewer: I'm talking to Jackie Gould, who's a very proud mother. Both of her daughters – Olivia, aged 12, and Alicia, seven – are currently appearing on the stage of the world-famous London Palladium theatre, in the musical *The Sound of Music*. Olivia and Alicia survived six auditions to be picked from 1,000 hopefuls for the group of seven children playing the Von Trapp family in the show. So how did it all come about?

Jackie: Well, until last year, the idea of them appearing at the London Palladium would have been unthinkable for our family. Things started to happen when Olivia auditioned for a production of the show *Annie* at the local theatre. She auditioned for the chorus and, by chance, got the leading role instead.

Interviewer: That's a very big role, the leading one in *Annie*, isn't it?

Jackie: Yes, for *Annie*, Olivia had to learn more than 200 lines. She was on stage for most of the two-hour show. It was a big script, and I decided that we'd do ten pages a night. After memorizing it, I gave her a random line. She would have to tell me what the next line was. She picked it all up even better than her homework.

Interviewer: And she did well in the part, presumably?

Jackie: She was great in the part. Everyone was astonished by her performance, including us. She had always been very shy, and she suddenly came out of her shell. We found that she could really sing. A member of the stage management team for the show was taking over a local agency and asked her to sign up. So then she had an agent to represent her and try to get roles for her.

Interviewer: OK, so what happened next?

Jackie: Well, Olivia was turned down for a part in the musical *Mary Poppins*. She reached the last ten for the role of Jane Banks. She didn't get the part and was distraught. But she quickly picked herself up and then we took both children to the Palladium auditions for *The Sound of Music*.

Interviewer: What was that like?

Jackie: Well, we arrived for the auditions at 8.30 a.m., as instructed, only to find a huge crowd ahead of us. Eventually, more than 1,000 children turned up. They said at first that they could only see 230 kids. We were at about number 250 and, with a visit to our local festival planned for the next day, we couldn't come back. We begged them to see our daughters and eventually they agreed.

Interviewer: And it went well?

Jackie: Both girls sang 'Over The Rainbow' for the producers and a week later they were told they had passed the initial hurdle. Their first call-back involved singing the harmonies for the title theme, as well as the song 'The Lonely Goatherd' from the show. I helped them rehearse by playing the tunes on our old upright piano in our dining room. They really worked hard and decided that for all auditions they would wear what they felt were their lucky clothes. Alicia had on a skirt and top and some dolly shoes. Olivia wore three-quarter length trousers, a stripy T-shirt and dolly shoes.

Interviewer: So they got through that audition?

Jackie: Yes, and for the next one they had to read some poetry, and eventually they got to the sixth and final one. It was all quite tense at the last audition. Alicia was already set to appear in a local show, so she was not openly worried, and Olivia joked that if she was rejected she could still sell programmes at the show. I impressed upon them that they need not worry if they were rejected, as much depended on whether their faces fitted, or they were the right height. I told them it was all down to luck.

Interviewer: But they passed, and now they're in the show. They must be thrilled.

Jackie: Yes. But it hasn't gone to their heads. I've told them both they're very lucky, and if all fails, life will go on as usual. They're both quite quiet, not show-offs, and they've got their feet firmly on the ground.

Interviewer: Well, wish them good luck from me.

Jackie: I will. Thanks.

In the exam you will hear the recording twice. To listen again now, go to the beginning of the track.

That is the end of Part Four.

TEST 4

Part One
You will hear people talking in eight different situations. For questions 1–8, choose the best answer, A, B or C.

ONE.

You hear someone talking on a radio programme. What is the speaker doing?

A recommending that listeners make a certain drink
B explaining why a drink is becoming more popular
C telling listeners about a drink they may not know about

Woman: Fresh lime soda is made by the side of the road in Calcutta, India. Citrus drinks are popular all over India but fresh lime soda is a speciality in Calcutta. Stallholders set up early in the morning, making the drink with fresh limes, soda water, sugar, a pinch of salt and freshly ground cumin. In hot weather, the body loses a lot of its salt through perspiration, so salty drinks, especially those with lime juice, are very refreshing. Limes grow easily in India and are used in numerous recipes. *repeat extract 1*

TWO.

You hear someone talking about people who travel a lot when they're young. What is his attitude towards these people?

A He is envious of them for having the opportunity.
B He feels that they are simply wasting their time.
C He can't understand why they do it.

Man: Of course these days there are lots of young people who spend a period of time travelling all over the world. We couldn't do that when I was younger – you couldn't get to all these places so easily and we didn't have the time or the money. But I don't feel like I've missed out at all. I mean, what do they actually see and learn? It seems to me that they just do it for the sake of it, as if they're just ticking places off on a list. They just do it because it's what people do. They can't be bothered to find out about the people or their culture. They just want to talk about where they've been when they get back. *repeat extract 2*

THREE.

You hear an advertisement for a course. What does the speaker say about the course?

A You need to take a test before being accepted for it.
B It starts with theory and moves on to practical work.
C It focuses on your effect on the people you will instruct.

Woman: Our Gym Instructor course will help you gain the skills and knowledge you need to get the best out of people and help them reach their fitness goals. On successful completion of the course, you'll be able to take the practical assessment test to prove that you've reached a recognized standard in working with people of different fitness levels and abilities. As well as studying anatomy and physiology, you'll learn about the importance of customer care and correct exercise technique. *repeat extract 3*

FOUR.

You hear part of a radio interview. Who is being interviewed?

A   a film director

B   an actor

C   a screenwriter

Interviewer: Do you ever add your own bits to a scene?

Man: I think with everything you do, you have the basic structure, but you do your best to explore it as much as possible while you're shooting a film. If you do something on the spur of the moment, it can be fun. You see the reactions all around. People panic for a second.

Interviewer: A lot of your characters have been pretty strange, haven't they?

Man: Are you saying I'm weird? Well, I think everyone's nuts, I really do. The strangest people in the world are the ones who are super-serious. They're probably crazier than any of the guys I've played. *repeat extract 4*

FIVE.

You hear part of a radio report about car drivers. What did the survey discover about a lot of drivers?

A   They pay no attention to warning lights.

B   They don't know what various symbols in a car relate to.

C   They think there are too many warning lights and symbols in cars.

Reporter: The meanings of symbols on dashboards are beyond the grasp of many drivers, a survey shows. Almost half of women and a third of men surveyed by the Automobile Association could not correctly identify symbols for frequently-used functions or basic warning lights. Researchers found that nearly 40 per cent of women and 28 per cent of men were unable to correctly identify the warning lamp for the main beam headlight. Two thirds of women could not correctly identify the front windscreen washer and wipe symbol and one in five admitted that they had no idea what it signified. *repeat extract 5*

SIX.

You turn on the radio and hear part of a programme. What type of programme is it?

A   a review programme

B   a chat show

C   a phone-in

Woman: It would be very interesting to find out what he was trying to achieve on this latest CD, because it's totally different from his previous ones. He's given several interviews since it came out but he doesn't seem to want to discuss the thinking behind this extraordinary change of style. Of course, the fans will make their views clear – they'll either stick with him despite the sudden change or they just won't buy it. Personally, I think it's a very effective and powerful set of songs and he deserves praise for not just sticking with his tried and tested formula. It's certainly the best of the releases we've looked at so far. *repeat extract 6*

SEVEN.

You hear part of a radio play. Where is the scene taking place?

A   in a restaurant

B   in a car

C   in a house

Man: Look, I know you're upset, but let's not ruin the whole evening over this.

Woman: That's easy for you to say. You're not the one who's been insulted.

Man: I know, but just try to forget it. Let's go for our meal, just as we planned it and try to enjoy ourselves. I have booked a table after all.

Woman: No, I just can't face it. Turn around and take me back. I'm really not in the mood.

Man: Well, I'm hungry.

Woman: Go on your own, then. But drop me off first. I just want to be on my own. *repeat extract 7*

EIGHT.

You hear a woman talking about running. What aspect of running is she talking about?

A   her involvement in running over a period of time

B   why she finds running so enjoyable

C   the importance of running and training with others

Woman: At school and college, I used to belong to an athletics club and enthusiastically took part in cross-country races. But then for years I didn't really do any exercise. Then, eighteen months ago, I decided to get fit and stay fit, and I rediscovered the joys of running. I started training and was soon hooked on running again. I got a colleague to join me and she caught the running bug so badly that she even joined an athletics club! Seeing each other every day at work and discussing running kept us both motivated and I found it surprisingly easy to stick to my schedule of training in the gym and going out for road runs. *repeat extract 8*

That is the end of Part One. Now turn to Part Two.

You will hear an announcement about a competition. For questions 9–18, complete the sentences. You now have 45 seconds to look at Part 2.

Woman: So, are you thinking about that idea again? That absolute money-spinner, the ultimate business brainchild that could change your fortunes and transform your life forever? No, you think, it's impossible. People like you should stick to dreaming. But what if you were given a real chance to change your life and achieve that goal? How would you react if the support you need suddenly landed in your lap? Not in the form of a loan – but free. Well, now's your chance. In this competition, we're offering £100,000 to a budding entrepreneur. and there are no obligations other than that you have to use the money to follow through your idea. All you have to do is convince us that your plan is worth backing. The £100,000 prize is to help pay for your financial commitments while you pursue your goal.

The competition is open to a variety of ideas and people. Perhaps you have a particular skill that you know could be put to more effective use in a different sector or country. Perhaps, given the right backing, you could change hundreds of lives. Are you an engineer with an idea that could transform sanitation and bring clean water to Africa? Or an architect with a vision that could solve the problems in Britain's inner cities? Or are you a farmer who could teach the world's poorest people how to grow crops in the worst conditions? If you are any of these, you could win the competition and the prize money.

Here are the details for entering. If you phone, after leaving your name and address, you will have up to one minute to pitch your idea. If you choose to email, you will have to pitch your idea in no more than 100 words. There are three categories of entry, and you will have to choose one of them. The first category is for those with an innovative idea for a business offering a new product or service. The second is for those who plan to learn new skills by taking a course such as an MBA. The third is for those who want to use their skills to support a socially-responsible project. The winner will be chosen from across all three categories.

Now, there are some other very important details if you are thinking of going in for the competition. Only one entry per person is allowed – multiple entries are not permitted. If you make a mistake while delivering your pitch, you will not be allowed to call back and leave another entry. We suggest that you practise delivering your pitch before phoning. If it helps, write down a script and read that. And remember, you can't go over the time limit.

Our judges will be looking for a number of qualities when they make their decision. The best idea will have big potential and demonstrate a great deal of innovation. The judges will want to be sure that the idea, if it was carried out, would change the life of the entrant, and preferably the lives of others. Entrants must be able to demonstrate great passion for their project, with thought having been given to how it could be put into practice. The top 100 will then be whittled down to 10, who will be invited to present their ideas in person to a panel of judges. The winner will then be announced.

In the exam you will hear the recording twice. To listen again now, go to the beginning of the track.

That is the end of Part Two. Now turn to Part Three.

You will hear five different people talking about how they felt when they received an award. For questions 19–23, choose from the list A–F how each person felt. Use the letters only once. There is one extra letter which you do not need to use. You now have 30 seconds to look at Part Three.

Speaker 1: When I won the Best Actor award it was an extraordinary moment. There had been so many occasions when I'd thought I might win an award, only to find that someone else got it instead. So when I finally got it I was thrilled. It was a fantastic personal achievement but in fact the main thing in my mind was all the people who had helped me along the way. I thought about all of them and all the help they'd given me. I knew that without them I would never have won it. And I mentioned as many of them as I could in the time available.

Speaker 2: I guess that being voted Footballer of the Year went to my head. All I could think about was how well I'd done. Me, the best! I thought back to the early years of my career, which weren't so great and I felt fantastic. And it was all thanks to my own efforts, not because anyone had handed me anything on a plate. It had been a long, hard journey but I'd finally made it to the very top. I suppose it made me a bit big-headed for a while, but I just felt so good about myself and what I'd managed to achieve.

Speaker 3: Everybody was expecting me to win the Writer of the Year award – I don't know why, there were plenty of other good contenders on the shortlist. Because everyone was predicting I'd win, I felt under pressure, as if it would be some kind of failure if I didn't win. It was a silly way to feel, I know, but I couldn't help it. So when my name was announced I was just glad that it was over and I had in fact won it. All the pressure came off me in a moment and I just felt like sitting down quietly rather than celebrating.

Speaker 4: These awards mean a lot in the music business and so winning the Best Singer award was a great honour. I'd worked so hard over the years and I'd spent so long getting nowhere that it was amazing to have achieved this recognition. I thought I'd be absolutely overcome with joy, but in fact the reverse happened. As I accepted the award, I was wondering if it would be all downhill from there. Would I be able to keep it up and stay at the top? Or would this be the high point, followed by a lot of low points? I couldn't put those thoughts out of my mind.

Speaker 5: I wasn't totally surprised when I got the Best Student award, because to be honest I felt that I deserved it. In fact, I'd put in so much effort to win it, doing far more work than anyone else, that I was completely worn out. It had been so important to me to win it that I'd dedicated myself completely to the task of winning it. So when I went up to collect it, I'd used up all my energy over the previous couple of weeks and was totally drained. I could barely put a few sentences together for my acceptance speech, though I managed to remember to thank a few people for their help.

In the exam you will hear the recording twice. To listen again now, go to the beginning of the track.

That is the end of Part Three. Now turn to Part Four.

You will hear an interview with someone who has started a magazine for children. For questions 24–30, choose the best answer, A, B or C. You now have one minute to look at Part Four.

Interviewer: It's tough maintaining a child's interest, but Kate Scarborough has had the experience to know what it's all about. Kate, you used to be a teacher, didn't you?

Kate: Yes, six years ago I had the idea that I wanted to do something for children, so I decided to be a primary school teacher. I have never been so tired as I was working as a teacher in a classroom. You just never stop. Working with children is so intensely exhausting, but it's also fantastic.

Interviewer: Well, today, we're sitting in your London office and talking about something very different – being the founder of *CY* magazine, a new magazine for children. Having worked in children's non-fiction publishing for 12 years before retraining as a primary school teacher, you certainly have the background to produce such a magazine.

Kate: Yes, well being a teacher I guess led me to the idea for *CY*. I felt that there was a gap in the market for a monthly publication that not only entertains and teaches children, but also satisfies their parents too. And it was during my teaching days that I began preparing for *CY*. I talked to children about what they wanted. I then thought, if I was a child, what would I want, and as a parent, what would I want my children to be reading?

Interviewer: OK, now the outcome is a magazine that's filled with competitions, short stories, puzzles, and a cartoon strip. Flicking through the first issue, I'd say

two things become apparent – enthusiasm and the language used.

Kate: Enthusiasm is incredibly important. When I was at school, it didn't matter what you were teaching children if you totally believed in it. When you give a bad lesson, you can see those blank faces looking back at you. I really hope I get that belief across, and that children find it entertaining and become interested in what's going on around them all the time.

Interviewer: How about the actual style of writing itself?

Kate: The whole brief to my writers was that they should approach it as if they are talking to intelligent people. Of course, you can't use some words because they would go above children's heads. But when I was doing my research, I put a number of texts in front of children. They are very perceptive – if they feel they are being talked down to, they see it. So it's all written in a direct way, rather than assuming you have to use a very childish style – the readers wouldn't like that.

Interviewer: Now, the age range for the magazine is stated as seven to 12 years, but it's quite difficult to judge that, isn't it?

Kate: Yes, children develop at different rates. For some at seven it will be difficult, but for others perfect. And when some hit 12 they become interested in totally different things. Parents will know whether or not it's right for their children.

Interviewer: Now a very interesting aspect of the magazine is its use of the Internet. Tell me about that.

Kate: Well, if children read something that interests them, by visiting the magazine's website they can learn much more about it. The reasons for this are rooted in my experiences at school. Take explorers as a subject. There are so many fantastic stories attached to them and all kinds of themes to raise excitement, but you can't spend a week teaching them that. So I wanted readers to be able to follow up a subject, in a way they may not be able to at school.

Interviewer: Now obviously, you want the magazine to be successful and profitable, I assume?

Kate: Yes, but ultimately, it isn't making a profit that's on my mind. I want to inspire children. If a child reads an article in the magazine on houses, for example, and they are inspired to go on to be an architect, that's great. It can be the tiniest thing that sparks a child off. From my point of view, I am trying to cover as much as I can so there's a chance of that little spark.

Interviewer: OK, now another aspect of the magazine .... (fade)

In the exam you will hear the recording twice. To listen again now, go to the beginning of the track.

That is the end of Part Four.

Paper 5: Speaking

PART 2

- What are the people trying to do?

- Whose rooms do you think these are?

PARTS 3 AND 4

- How popular would these suggestions for new exhibitions be?
- Which two would attract the most visitors?

Paper 5: Speaking

<u>PART 2</u>

■ What are the characteristics of each kind of film?

1A

1B

■ What do you think the situation is?

2A

2B

- How attractive would these special days be as a prize?
- Which one should be the prize?

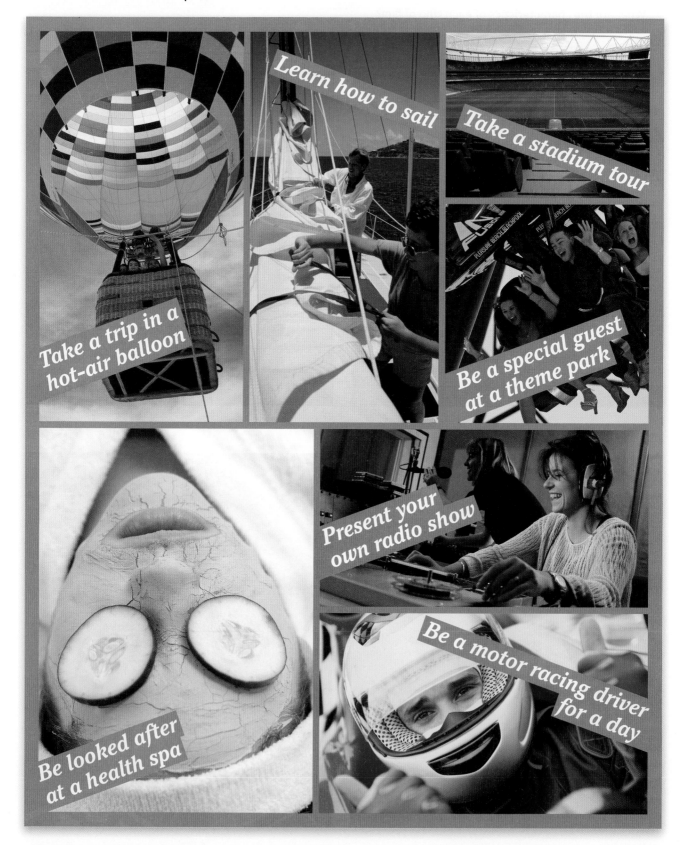

Paper 5: Speaking

PART 2

■ Why do you think the person is taking the photograph?

■ What is the situation in each photograph?

PARTS 3 AND 4

- What should be included in the one-day festival?
- Where should each one be?

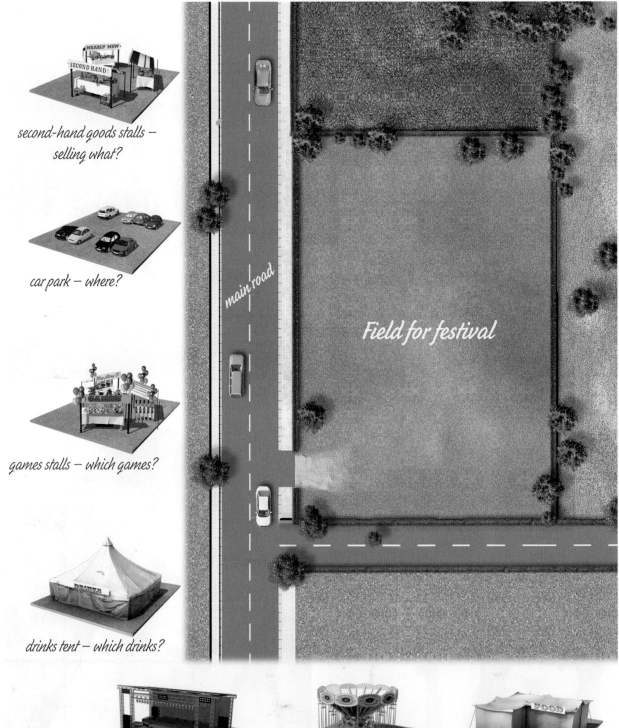

second-hand goods stalls – selling what?

car park – where?

games stalls – which games?

drinks tent – which drinks?

main road

Field for festival

stage for musical performances (to be built)

small rides – what kind?

food tent – what kind of food?